In this book, Iliana Zloch-Christy analyses the problems of Eastern Europe's convertible currency external debt situation and its impact on the financing of East–West trade in the late 1980s and early 1990s. This is a continuation of Dr Zloch-Christy's *Debt problems of Eastern Europe* (1987) and is the first study of the present day complexities of East–West trade and finance.

The author addresses four main issues. First, she examines the recent market-oriented reforms in Eastern Europe's economic system and the changes that have taken place in East–West political relations. Dr. Zloch-Christy then assesses whether convertible currency debt problems are an inherent part of the economic development of Eastern Europe, and if the problems are region-wide, and she discusses the strategies adopted to deal with them. She continues by exploring the extent to which the problems arising from indebtedness have affected the financing of East–West trade. Commercial and production compensation, various forms of credit and funding from international financial institutions are the main financial arrangements discussed. Finally, the author assesses medium- and long-term debt prospects both for Eastern Europe as a whole and for each country within the CMEA.

East–West financial relations: Current problems and future prospects is an important and highly topical study of the CMEA external balance and East–West trade and credit relations. It will be of interest to students and specialists of Soviet and East European studies, international finance and economics. It will also be an important reference work for government agencies and international financial institutions.

EAST-WEST FINANCIAL RELATIONS

Soviet and East European Studies

80 ILIANA ZLOCH-CHRISTY
East–West financial relations
Current problems and future prospects

79 MICHAEL D. KENNEDY
Professionals, power and Solidarity in Poland
A critical sociology of Soviet-type society

78 GARETH M. WINROW
The foreign policy of the GDR in Africa

77 JOZEF M. VAN BRABANT
The planned economies and international economic organizations

76 WILLIAM MOSKOFF
The bread of affliction: the food supply in the USSR during World War II

75 YAACOV RO'I
The struggle for Soviet-Jewish emigration 1948–1967

74 GRAEME GILL
The origins of the Stalinist political system

73 SANTOSH MEHROTRA
India and the Soviet Union: trade and technology transfer

72 ILYA PRIZEL
Latin America through Soviet eyes
The evolution of Soviet perceptions during the Brezhnev era 1964–1982

71 ROBERT G. PATMAN
The Soviet Union in the Horn of Africa
The diplomacy of intervention and disengagement

70 IVAN T. BEREND
The Hungarian economic reforms 1953–1988

69 CHRIS WARD
Russia's cotton workers and the New Economic Policy
Shop-floor culture and state policy 1921–1929

68 LÁSZLÓ CSABA
Eastern Europe in the world economy

67 MICHAEL E. URBAN
An algebra of Soviet power
Elite circulation in the Belorussian Republic 1966–1986

66 JANE L. CURRY
Poland's journalists: professionalism and politics

65 MARTIN MYANT
The Czechoslovak economy 1948–1988
The battle for economic reform

64 XAVIER RICHET
The Hungarian model: markets and planning in a socialist economy

63 PAUL G. LEWIS
Political authority and party secretaries in Poland 1975–1986

EAST–WEST FINANCIAL RELATIONS

Current problems and future prospects

ILIANA ZLOCH-CHRISTY

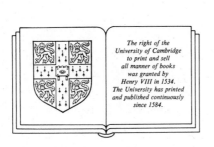

The right of the
University of Cambridge
to print and sell
all manner of books
was granted by
Henry VIII in 1534.
The University has printed
and published continuously
since 1584.

CAMBRIDGE UNIVERSITY PRESS

Cambridge
New York   Port Chester
Melbourne   Sydney

9100019432

Published by the Press Syndicate of the University of Cambridge
The Pitt Building, Trumpington Street, Cambridge CB2 1RP
40 West 20th Street, New York, NY 10011, USA
10 Stamford Road, Oakleigh, Melbourne 3166, Australia

First published 1991

Printed in Great Britain at the University Press, Cambridge

British Library cataloguing in publication data
Zloch-Christy, Iliana
East–West financial relations: current problems and
future prospects. – (Soviet and East European Studies)
1. Western bloc countries. Economic relations with Eastern
Europe 2. Europe. Eastern Europe. Economic relations with
Western Bloc countries
I. Title II. Series
377.4701713

Library of Congress cataloguing in publication data
Zloch-Christy, Iliana, 1953–
East–West financial relations: current problems and future
prospects/Iliana Zloch-Christy.
    p.   cm. – (Soviet and East European studies: 80)
Includes index.
ISBN 0 521 39530 5
1. Debts, External – Europe, Eastern. 2. East–West trade (1945-)
3. Foreign exchange problem – Europe, Eastern. I. Title.
II. Series.
HJ8615.Z573   1991
336.3'435'0947 – dc20   90–1898   CIP

ISBN 0 521 39530 5 hardback

CE

To my mother and
my father

Contents

List of figures	page	x
List of tables		xi
Acknowledgements		xii
List of abbreviations		xiii
Introduction		1
1 Eastern Europe in a time of change		3
2 The Eastern European external debt situation		30
3 The financing of East–West trade		51
4 Medium- and long-term debt prospects in Eastern Europe		77
Conclusion		101
Epilogue		103
Notes		107
References		116
Index		120

Figures

1 Soviet foreign trade system   page 23
2 Barter   54
3 Counterpurchase   55
4 Switch   65
5 Triangular compensation   66
6 Forfeiting deal   69

Tables

1 Economic reform, 1989   17
2 CMEA current account balances with market economies, 1980–1987   31
3 Annual changes in value of East–West trade, 1983–1987   33
4 Changes in terms of trade in East–West trade, 1983–1987   33
5 Eastern European convertible-currency gross debt, 1980–1988   34
6 Eastern European convertible-currency net debt, 1980–1988   35
7 Medium and long-term funds raised by Eastern European countries on the international financial markets, 1980–1988   37
8 Terms of syndicated credits to Eastern Europe, 1980–1988   38
9 CMEA debt service ratios, 1980–1988   39
10 CMEA net debt/exports ratios, 1980–1988   39
11 CMEA liquidity ratios, 1980–1988   40
12 Eastern Europe's securities offerings in 1984–1988   75

Acknowledgements

This monograph presents a continuation of my book on *Debt Problems of Eastern Europe* published few years ago. I prepared the new study during my research fellowship in St Antony's College, Oxford. The fascinating intellectual atmosphere of Oxford was a great stimulus for my work.

I am very grateful to Joe Berliner, Frank Holzman and Michael Kaser for carefully reviewing an earlier draft, and for making constructive and stimulating suggestions for improvement. Mark Allen, Daniel Bond, Helmut Haschek, Ed Hewett, John M. Howell, Peter Lucas, Paul Lendvai, Mario Nuti, Chandra Pant, Richard Portes and Jeffrey Sachs provided helpful advice. I benefited from the discussions with participants of the economic seminar in St Antony's, at seminars at Harvard University, and also at the European University Institute in Florence. The seminars at the World Bank and in the Research Department of the International Monetary Fund were very useful in completing my work.

For financial support in preparing the study I would like to thank the British Council, the Austrian Girozentrale Bank, the Austrian Kontrollbank, the Austrian FWF, and the Woodrow Wilson International Centre for Scholars in Washington, D.C.

Finally, a word of gratitude to my parents. They inspired my interest in economics and without their generous understanding, my studies and work over the years in Bulgaria, Austria, USA and United Kingdom would not have been possible.

Abbreviations

BIS	Bank for International Settlements
CMEA	Council for Mutual Economic Assistance
CPE	centrally planned economies
DME	developed market economies
ECE	Economic Commission for Europe
EC	European Community
EFTA	European Free Trade Association
EIB	European Investment Bank
IBEC	International Bank for Economic Cooperation
IBRD	International Bank for Reconstruction and Development
EIB	European Investment Bank
GATT	General Agreement on Tariffs and Trade
GDP	gross domestic product
GNP	gross national product
IMF	International Monetary Fund
LDC	less developed country
LIBOR	London interbank offered rate
NIC	newly industrialized country
NMP	net material product
OECD	Organization for Economic Cooperation and Development
OPEC	Organization of Petroleum Exporting Countries
SDR	special drawing rights
UN	United Nations
UNCTAD	United Nations Conference on Trade and Development
WEFA	Wharton Econometric Forecasting Associates

Introduction

This study analyses the problems of Eastern Europe's[1] convertible currency external debt situation and its impact on the financing of East–West trade in the late 1980s and in the 1990s. A discussion of the present CMEA economic reforms provides the background for this approach to East–West financial relations. Throughout the study I seek more to raise relevant questions with appropriate background information, rather than to draw specific conclusions. In this book I do not aim to project on the basis of a computer model Eastern Europe's trade balances, current account balances and balances of payments, as I did recently (Zloch-Christy 1986, 1988), but to present an analytical framework for a discussion on the present and future trends in the CMEA external balance and East–West trade and credit relations. The study addresses the following questions:

1 What are the main trends in reforming Eastern Europe's economic system and in the East–West political dialogue?
2 Were convertible-currency debt difficulties inherent in the economic development of Eastern Europe in the late 1980s?
3 How the problems arising from indebtedness have affected the financing of East–West trade and what are the main financing forms?
4 What are the medium and long-term debt prospects?

The structure of the study is as follows. Chapter 1 explores the changes in Eastern Europe envisaged by the recent reforms. It focuses on the economic and political aspects of *perestroika*, reforming the foreign trade mechanism and the concept of capital markets in Eastern Europe. Chapters 2, 3 and 4 turn specifically to the discussion of Eastern European debt and forms of financing East–West trade. Chapter 2 examines debt trends in the second half of the 1980s, asking three main questions.

1 Is there a regionwide debt problem in Eastern Europe?

1

2 How realistic is it to expect that Poland and Hungary will restore their creditworthiness in the medium term?

3 What are the creditor–debtor policy strategies in the East–West financial relations?

Chapter 3 concerns the forms of financing East–West trade. It examines commercial compensation (countertrade – barter, counter-purchase, buy-back deals – and multilateral trade accords), production compensation (joint ventures, cooperation agreements), financial compensation (clearing/switch and 'transit' deals, export-leasing, export-factoring, and forfeiting), and some other forms of financing: supplier's credits, project financing, lines of credit, free credits, funds from international financial institutions, and Eastern Europe's access to the international securities markets. Chapter 4 analyses the prospects for East European debt in the 1990s, collectively and by country. The analysis focuses on the following questions: What will be the impact of the economic reforms on the CMEA external balance and creditworthiness? How can effects of the reform changes be assessed? What are the main issues related to political risk assessment in lending to Eastern Europe? What are the alternative scenarios for debt developments and what is the likelihood of debt servicing difficulties in the region? The main findings of the study are summarised in the conclusion.

The first draft of the study was completed in early 1989. Since then rapid changes have occurred in the political and economic life of Eastern Europe, with the events of late 1989 and 1990. The revisions of the study in March 1990 discuss these developments. However, despite all these changes, the general conclusions of the book still stand.

1   Eastern Europe in a time of change

Since 1985 Eastern Europe has been attempting to reform the centrally planned economic system. The present reforms are regarded by East European and Western scholars, businessmen and officials as the most radical reforms in the history of the CMEA economic mechanism in the recent thirty years. This chapter discusses the economic and political aspects of 'perestroika' and the main developments in reforming the foreign trade system and in creating capital markets in Eastern Europe.

Economic and political aspects of *perestroika*

The frequency of attempts to reform the CMEA centrally planned economic system and their reversal after the mid-1950s indicate the intensive pressure for change and the difficulty of its successful implementation. The present round of reforms involves the Soviet Union and four other Eastern European countries – Bulgaria, Czechoslovakia, Hungary and Poland. There are no signs of reform in the GDR and Romania. In the GDR the pressure for reform at present is considerably reduced by its 'special relationship' with West Germany and by its flexible vertically integrated economic structure. The GDR foreign trade system is decentralized and collectives play an important role in agriculture. However, the reunification of Germany in October 1990 puts the discussion on economic reform in East Germany in a completely different light from the reforms in the other East European countries. Romania is still firmly continuing to resist any change in its highly centralised economic bureaucratic system.

Pillars of the reform

The present reforms[1] aim not only at changing priorities and changing policies as previous attempts did, but at changing the economic system. The following are the three main pillars of the reform process:

1 privatisation (to a certain point) of the means of production and diversification of the forms of economic activity;
2 decentralisation of management decision making in the economy;
3 reducing the political monopoly of the single party.

Cooperatives, private enterprises (small businesses and services) and the quasi-private sector (leaseholds, e.g. in agriculture) are steps towards privatisation of the state means of production. Horizontal relations in the economy are meant to replace the vertical centrally planned economic structure and market signals are expected to guide the behaviour of economic subjects. The terms 'self-dependence', 'self-financing' and 'self-management' characterise the main directions of the decentralisation of decision making in Eastern Europe. The reforms aim also at creating political liberalisation – openness (*glasnost*), more democratic rights and even multiparty systems in the societies of the Soviet Union and East Europe dominated by the monopoly power of a single political party for more than forty years.

The Soviet economist Aganbegyan (1989: 1) defines the process of *perestroika* as follows:

> The main aim is to change the economic management of our country from the administrative ('diktat' or command) system developed over the last fifty years to a radically new one based on economic levers such as market forces, financial credits, and other stronger economic stimuli. The whole process must be carried out alongside a general democratisation of our society and a transition to self-administration in our enterprises.

The main directions of the economic and political reforms in Eastern Europe indicate that these countries are facing changes which were not anticipated by Eastern and Western scholars and politicians in 1985. Scholars did not predict the political and social changes; all of the communist Eastern European governments could not control them. Even the most pessimistic and conservative observers agree that Eastern Europe is undergoing a dramatic period of change. There are two major differences between the present reforms and all of the previous reform attempts. It is stressed by the Eastern European policy makers (particularly in the Soviet Union, Poland and Hungary) that in the first place, economic reform will not succeed without political reform and therefore the two reforms must be simultaneously carried out; and, in the second, the CMEA command economies must be restructured from 'top to bottom'. In the Soviet Union many scholars and politicians stress that the process of Gorbachev's *perestroika* policy is democratisation plus economic reform.[2] *Perestroika* is a revolution (in the sense of a decisive break with the past) against the socialist model established more than sixty years ago.[3] Gorbachev's policy is a policy of 'new realism' in a world of interdependence.[4]

Why 'perestroika'?

The Soviet academician Aganbegyan answers the question of why *perestroika* as follows: 'The old economic structure, the old patterns of development, did not correspond to the new conditions both inside the Soviet Union and internationally ... It became very clear that it was insufficient to make minor changes in the running of the economy. New, radical reform – a "restructuring" – was needed' (Aganbegyan, 1988a, p. 41). Gorbachev said at the June 1987 plenum of the Central Committee that the economy was in a pre-crisis situation and essential restructuring was the only way to avert the crisis. He stated several times that if he had to go back to run the Soviet Union by the old methods he would 'not run it at all' (*The Economist*, 7 October 1989, p. 58).

It took the Soviet Union more than seventy years and the other Eastern European countries more than forty years to distance themselves from the Marxist–Leninist doctrine and to replace it with a pragmatic attitude towards economic and political life. It is interesting to mention here the statement by J. M. Keynes more than half a century ago (in the first years of the Soviet state): 'How can I accept a doctrine which sets up as its bible, above and beyond criticism, an obsolete economic textbook which I know to be not only scientifically erroneous but without interest or application for the modern world?' (Keynes, 1963, p. 300).

It is more widely understood in the Soviet Union and Eastern Europe at present that in the era of the 'third industrial revolution' (modern technology and information-based economy) technological and sectoral restructuring of the national economies is necessary and that abandoning traditional policies of over-ambitious investment and unconditional commitment to price stability and full employment are needed. The economic reforms encourage a greater opening to direct foreign trade with CMEA countries, less developed countries (LDCs) and developed market economies, foreign investment and activating of money and monetary policy to be followed by an establishment of capital markets. Commercial banks, leasing, bonds, shares, auctions, interest rates policy, market clearing prices, convertibility, are some of the radical new terms in the terminology of the present economic reforms as compared to the previous reform attempts. The problem of currency convertibility is regarded to be one of serious consideration for policy-makers and scholars. All of this indicates that (at least in the reform documents) the reforms in the Soviet Union and Eastern Europe have passed the stage of really radical reform and orthodox communist ideology.

Reform dilemmas

There are two major reform dilemmas: firstly, macroeconomic adjustment versus institutional change, and secondly, partial or overall, one-stroke or successive reform. Economic theory and the experience of the reforming centrally planned economies in Eastern Europe do not suggest a clear answer to the question of how to approach these dilemmas. The first dilemma is connected with the various serious imbalances (or, using the Kornai term, 'shortages'), both past and present, in the CMEA economies; on the one hand, chronic excess demand, repressed or open inflation, and, even unemployment in some of them, and on the other hand, trade deficits, balance of payments deficits and external debt. The approach of the reformers to this dilemma is to introduce much more decentralisation, encourage more reliance on market forces, more competition, liberalisation and deregulation.

The second dilemma concerns the speed and the scope of the reform. The reform process in the Eastern European countries is an experiment *in vivo*. Repeated revisions of the programmes regarding the speed and scope of the reforms can be observed (e.g. price reforms) and probably will be required in the future. However, life proves that CMEA economic reforms associated with gradual modification of the economic system are self-defeating.

Some of the Eastern European countries (Poland) decided in late 1989 for an on-stroke reform with a rapid move towards a market economy. Hungary, on the other hand, decided in the past twenty years (since its reform process began) on gradual and non-simultaneous radical changes in economic mechanism and economic policies. It is interesting to mention here the statement made recently by the Hungarian economist J. Kornai (1990, p. 90) that he firmly believes that the Hungarian people 'would prefer to face a single radical shock and the ensuing trauma if they were really convinced that the situation would improve as a result, rather than to suffer the hopeless torture, the slow but steady economic deterioration and the economic and social spasms we are now undergoing'. The main problems to be solved in connection with the second dilemma are ownership (allowing the existence of various forms of state and non-state owned firms), abolishing the mandatory short-term output targets and input quotas for the firms, direct privatisation, and the transformation of the state-owned enterprises into truly market-oriented economic units. The principal approach of the reformers to this dilemma is reliance on the exchange rate, fiscal and monetary policies, price and wage control, freedom for the different forms of ownership to compete with each other, autonomy and full responsibility of firms, abolishment of subsidies, bankruptcy law, and import liberalisation.

Reform in the Eastern European countries

The individual Eastern European countries differ in their specific goals and in the scope of economic reform. The Soviet Union's reforms seek to solve three sets of problems: the growing technological gap with the Western industrialised countries; low efficiency in the use of factors of production, capital, labour and land; and, welfare in the sense of the improving and correcting of incentives, social consumption, etc. The foundation of the new policy in the Soviet Union is the condemnation of the previous Soviet leaders for the purblindness they had induced in themselves and inflicted on a good part of Soviet society; they were out of touch with reality, their vision being obscured by archaic formulae and outworn dogmas.

The 'New Economic Mechanism' of June 1987 aims to improve the efficient use of factors of capital, labour and land by greater use of 'market relations'. Central planning is expected to be restricted to the macroeconomic level. The branch industries will have fewer directive functions and the state firms, collective firms, individual and collective businesses will have more autonomy. Competition, profit-motive, greater sensitivity to the conditions of supply and demand are expected to guide the behaviour of firms. The number of Soviet cooperatives increased in 1988 from 14,000 to 77,500, i.e. more than 5 times; 1.4 million people are employed in the cooperatives (*The Financial Times*, 19 April 1989, p. 2). The foreign trade system was liberalised and possibilities for foreign investments and openness to foreign competition were created (see p. 22). The industrial reform (Law on the enterprises of June 1987 and January 1988) envisaged four major departures from past practice: from January 1988 the rate of profit tax was set for the enterprises on a medium-term basis and the greater part of the profit remains with the enterprises; a number of new banks were established in August 1987, which can lend money to the firms; bankruptcy regulations have been in force from January 1988; reform of wholesale and retail prices was expected to be carried out in the medium term. The agricultural reform envisages decentralisation, decollectivisation, the encouraging of the 'contract brigade system' (a brigade's membership, leader and work schedules are self-chosen) and the establishment of some new type agricultural firms (cooperatives in the urban areas, free farmers – families or individuals – and others). At the March 1989 plenum of the Central Committee, Gorbachev stressed again the importance of leasehold tenure of land (for fifty years) for the entire agrarian sector as a major impulse to revitalise Soviet agriculture and increase its productivity. In the second half of 1989 the Soviet government introduced one of the most radical experiments in agriculture by promising to pay farms in hard currency for any grain and oil-seed production above recent average levels. This is an attempt to encourage farmers to produce more and to reduce food imports at some point, and ease the shortage of foreign exchange. The purchasing system will be introduced in 1990 and 1991. Soviet farms will have the right to spend the earned hard currency free from government intervention (*The Financial Times*, 11 August 1989, p. 1).

The reform-minded Soviet economists initiated numerous meetings with leading Western businessmen and scholars from 1986 onwards. Some of these meetings were consultations, in 1989, with the West German government regarding its experience in introducing convertibility of the D-Mark in 1958, and consultations with the chairman of the American Federal Reserve Board, Alan Greenspan, in Moscow in October 1989 (*The Economist*, 14 October 1989, p. 60).

One of the most radical reform-minded Soviet economists, Academician Oleg Bogomolov, stated that the reformers were no longer satisfied with half measures: half market, half plan. Their goal is a 'proper transition to the market'. He stressed further that the attempts should be oriented not at democratic decoration of the existing order but at genuine democracy which will allow the Soviet people to express their will and to know the truth about past and present (*The Economist*, 16 September 1989, p. 52). These radical views were reflected in several new laws discussed by the Soviet parliament in late 1989 and introduced in early 1990; some of these laws are property law allowing the existence of republic, cooperative, joint venture, and shareholding property and limiting the role of the state in the liquidation and reorganisation of enterprises; the law on leasing which might lead to a rapid expansion of leasing in the Soviet economy during the 1990s; a new land law encouraging (among other things) leasing in agriculture; and a law on republic and regional autonomy. For the first time in the history of the Soviet Union, radical deputies are preparing the draft of a bill which would legalise a multiparty system and multiparty elections (*The Financial Times*, 26 September 1989, p. 2). At the local elections in Moscow in March 1990 several new political groups participated. It is interesting to note that approximately 70 per cent of the candidates were party members but the ruling communist party was not registered. There is no doubt that in the Soviet parliament the so-called Inter-Regional Group, an opposition group headed by a five-man leadership, including the radical reformer Boris Yeltzin, will increase its influence.

As regards the reforms in the smaller Eastern European countries, let me begin with Czechoslovakia, the first CMEA country to attempt to introduce liberalisation of its economy in the mid-1960s. The present reform in Czechoslovakia hardly resembles at all the revolutionary 1968 reform (which had its origin in a Central Committee decision of early 1965)[5] and does not depart from policies which maintain the 'happy' stagnation (low but stable rates of economic growth and no large domestic and external imbalances) of the last twenty years or more. The law on central planning from mid-1989 indicates that efforts are not focused towards market-oriented economic reform. The present Soviet type practice of self-finance ('full *khozraschet*') came into force on 1 January 1989 (Law on the Enterprise from 1987). The main goals of the New Economic Mechanism are revision of the price system but with central price fixing continuing, reduction in the share of state orders, the phasing down of subsidies, rationalisation of the tax system, and introduction of a unified exchange rate (eliminating the difference between commercial and tourist rates). The government regulations of 1986 encourage establishment of joint ventures with Western and Eastern European countries. The first foreign exchange actions in which US dollars were sold at seven times the official rate took place in 1989 (IMF, *Morning Press*, External Relations Department, 1 September 1989). The 'Directive for Comprehensive Restructuring of the Economic Mechanism' envisages convertibility of the national currency and Czechoslovak scholars stress in their analysis that the need for convertibility both with CMEA countries and developed market economies 'is increasingly necessary'.[6]

The new 'political spring' in Czechoslovakia of late 1989 raises hopes not only for further liberalisation of political life but also for more radical steps towards liberalisation of the economy. The new government, however did not accept a programme in this regard after its election in late 1989.

The attempts to reform the economy radically and to democratise political life in Poland were strongly advanced with the establishment, in the second half of 1989, of the first non-communist government in Eastern Europe for more than forty years, led by Solidarity. In October 1989 the new government announced a plan for a radical economic liberalisation, which is a step further in implementing the goals of the previous reform programmes. Let me briefly discuss the main directions of the pre-Solidarity attempts at economic reform. The 1987 economic reform in Poland aimed at creating effective market relations between enterprises (state and non-state-owned). The firms are allowed to have considerable access to foreign markets. After the first wave of reform attempts in the early 1980s a substantial private sector has developed outside the state industries. The private sector dominates agriculture. The 1987 reform envisaged the further development of private firms in industry and trade and supported private agricultural units. A new law on enterprises came into force from 1 January 1989 which has created a favourable climate for the establishment of private firms. In the first two months of 1989 some 15,000 new private enterprises (handicrafts, services, trade and others) were registered (*Der Spiegel*, 20 February 1989, p. 143). The establishment of joint ventures with Western firms is strongly encouraged by the new reform (see chapter 3). From January 1989 foreign firms have been allowed to buy shares in Polish enterprises up to 100 per cent (*The Economist*, 17 February 1989, p. 19). State firms could, from June 1983, be declared bankrupt. The financial independence of state enterprises has been enhanced and they now have more authority over their revenues. New banks were created but state and private firms cannot obtain credits any more easily than in the past because the banks have little to lend. The state enterprises have to seek credit mainly through the supervising branch ministry. The tax reforms aimed at achieving uniform personal and corporation taxes and at shifting the tax burden towards value-added tax. The reform in the foreign trade system envisages (among other things) full convertibility of the zloty within the next three to five years, elimination of central allocation of foreign exchange, large-scale auctions of foreign exchange (from 1 April 1989) and even the establishment of retail foreign exchange businesses (*The Financial Times*, 14 February 1989, p. 2). The new Bank for Export Development organises auctions where state and private firms sell and buy hard currency at rates reflecting supply and demand (three times as high or more than the official rate). Author's estimates (Zloch-Christy), suggest that over 30 per cent of Polish hard currency imports in 1989 were financed through the auctions. The auctions have absorbed more than $US 2.5 billion (which is approximately half of the Polish export revenues in 1989). From 15 March 1989 private individuals and foreign tourists are allowed to trade hard currency among themselves legally at a free market rate (more than five times as high as the official rate). In 1989 private hard currency savings amounted to some $US 3 billion and annual remittances from abroad to about $US 1 billion (*The Financial Times*, 15 March 1989, p. 2).

The October 1989 economic plan envisages implementation of further major structural changes to be completed by early 1991. The main goals of the economic programme in implementation from 1 January 1990 are: first, the introduction of market-clearing prices determined in part on free trade with the West; second, the establishing and enlarging of the private sector by removing administrative restrictions; third, increasing the control and financial discipline ('hard budget constraint') over the large (state) sector by privatisation and by bankruptcy regulations; and fourth, maintaining overall macroeconomic stability through restrictive monetary and fiscal policies. The specific goals are a sharp reduction in the budget deficit, the establishment of a realistic unified exchange rate, implementation of income policies designed to restrain excessive wage increases, the removal of fiscal and administrative restrictions, and a reform of the tax system to encourage entrepreneurship. The plan aims more specifically at the abolition of administrative controls over prices, tight monetary policy and introduction of positive real interest rates, tight fiscal policy and elimination of individual tax reliefs, banking reform, more reduction of subsidies, reduction of government spending (police and military), privatisation of state enterprises, introduction of a new system of social insurance, an end to the monetisation of government debt and others. Cutting subsidies and reducing the budget deficit are designed to curb the inflationary pressures. A further devaluation of the zloty is planned in order to put the official rate of Polish currency on a par with the free market rate of foreign currencies (twelve devaluations were introduced from January to October 1989). Further goals of the economic plan are the establishment of a stock exchange by the end of 1990 and the introduction of value-added tax in 1991 (*The Financial Times*, 13 October 1989, p. 18; *The Economist*, 13 January 1990, p. 22).

The implementation of this plan will depend critically on Polish access to the international capital markets and funds from the IMF and the World Bank. The aid packages (including food) provided by several Western countries, including the FRG, the United Kingdom, France, the USA, Canada, and others in late 1989 were undoubtedly very important in avoiding a sharp drop in living standards. The discussions on measures to support economic and political liberalisation in Poland, Hungary and the other Eastern European countries (Bulgaria, Czechoslovakia, Romania), in the European Community, at the meetings of G-7 group in July and September 1989, and at the Annual Meetings of the IMF and the World Bank for Poland and Hungary in September 1989, give evidence that Western support would be expected for the efforts to restructure the Polish economy in the early 1990s.

Political reform at present is characterised by two main events: firstly, the legalising of Solidarity in April 1989 and the establishment of a Solidarity-led government, and secondly, the creation of a more democratic parliamentary system. The reform of the parliamentary system is designed to establish a new upper house of the parliament and a French-style presidency with powers to dissolve the lower house.

Hungary's economic reforms were the most farreaching in Eastern Europe during the 1980s. The 1968 reform allowed considerable flexibility in market relations among state-owned firms, private economic activity in services and small-scale production, foreign trade rights for domestic enterprises on a permit basis, joint ventures with foreign firms and more scope than anywhere in Eastern Europe for private activity in the collectivised agriculture. After 1979 two top-level committees, The Economic Committee and The State Planning Committee, were established in an effort to decentralise the macroeconomic management system. A further step to create only one industrial policymaker was the merging of the industrial branch ministries in 1982. Price reforms (wholesale and retail prices) were introduced and subsidisation of enterprise investment was reduced. There are plans to cut subsidies to firms and consumers by 50 per cent over the next three years. In January 1987 several competing banks were established. The reform of the banking system is oriented at creating and specifying the activities of three main groups of financial institutions: commercial banks, financial intermediaries dealing with specific financial tasks, and the central bank (responsible for the whole monetary sphere and the stability of the national currency). Bankruptcy regulations are in force within a general government policy of market surveillance.[7] One of the goals of the reformers is that all state enterprises are self-financing, with regulation of unfair trading practices and of monopolisation. Private, cooperative and concessionaire businesses have been encouraged. There are proposals for a direct privatisation in the economy in the early 1990s. The reform of taxation – an income tax and VAT instead of turnover tax – was farreaching in CMEA countries in the late 1980s. From January 1989 private firms are allowed to employ up to 500 people (previously 35). Foreign companies are allowed to buy stock in Hungarian firms up to 100 per cent (*The Economist*, 17 February 1989, p. 19). Since January 1989 joint ventures with less than 50 per cent foreign participation need no official registration. Hungary is the first East European country in which 'stock exchange days' are organised as an embryonic form of a real stock exchange to be established in 1989–90. The introduction of the convertibility of the currency is considered to be a very important tool for creating a competitive and efficient economy. The Hungarian finance minister stated that in contrast to Poland, Hungary wants 'to reach convertibility not by devaluations, but by a deflationary process' (*The New York Times*, 6 March 1990, p. D7).

Ideas for the democratisation of society in Hungary were (with those of Poland) the most farreaching in Eastern Europe in the 1980s before the radical changes in late 1989 in Bulgaria, Czechoslovakia, the GDR and Romania; however, in the case of the latter it is still not clear what the political determination is. The government has stated several times that the main goal in the late 1980s and in the 1990s is to create a free market multiparty state with Western aid, even if initially this transformation would cause social conflict (*The Financial Times*, 3 August 1989, p. 2). In early 1989 a party commission was set up in order to hold talks with some fifteen alternative political groups already in existence (the largest and most influential among them being the Hungarian Democratic Forum). An agreement on a new constitution and on the party role in the period 1990–5 (considered to be a 'transition period' between the two parliamentary elections in 1990 and 1995) was achieved in September 1989. It stipulates, for example, the direct election of the president before the free parliamentary elections to be held not later than ninety days after the presidential election, a new electoral law, and a depolitisation of the army (*The Financial Times*, 20 September 1989, p. 3). The Hungarian parliament adopted some 100 modifications to its constitution in 1989. Under the new constitution, Hungary will become a democratic republic asserting 'the values of both bourgeois democracy and democratic socialism' (IMF *Morning Press*, 19 October 1989). The transition sets the basis for the multiparty system, codifies human and civil rights, and separates the judicial, executive and legislative branches of government. The ruling communist party was renamed in October 1989 as the Hungarian Socialist Party in order to stress the distance from previous policies and the effort to be seen more as a Western style social democratic party than a traditional communist party. It is very probable that a non-communist government will be formed (as in Poland) after the elections in April 1990. The Social Democratic Forum accepted initially the proposal that the new prime minister after the elections was to be from the communist party. Later, however, this agreement was reconsidered by both sides and the Forum won the elections.

The Hungarian prime minister M. Nemeth stressed in an interview in 1989 that the major goals of the Hungarian reform are now 'peaceful transition to a democratic society'. He stated further that 'even if the Soviet reforms were to slow down, the Hungarian reforms would continue', because they are irreversible and have the full support of the people (*The Daily Telegraph*, 13 March 1989: 18).

Bulgaria's economic reform also demonstrates new approaches in dealing with the economic problems of the centrally planned economy and points the way to the farreaching changes, including self-management and decentralised banking, which have taken place since January 1988. Direct contacts between domestic enterprises and foreign firms have been encouraged; this is a further step to bring self-managing firms into direct contact with foreign markets. Foreign enterprises are allowed to buy a share, even a majority share in Bulgarian enterprises (decree of March 1980). Hard currency auctions have been organised since 1988. According to the 'Rulebook on Economic Activity' Bulgarian enterprises are allowed to keep part of their foreign currency revenues. However, in practice, these rules are not strictly followed. For some transitional years the domestic self-managing firms are required to conclude and give priority to the fulfilment of the so-called 'state orders'. However, they are allowed to conclude contracts on market terms with other firms and none may be refused if productive capacity is not fully utilised. The 1988 Bulgarian reform envisaged the introduction of the convertibility of the national currency, initially with the CMEA currencies.

The application of Bulgaria to join the Bretton Woods institutions in early 1990 indicates her determination for radical economic reforms. New political groups were established and the opposition had several discussions with the communist government which replaced in late 1989 the orthodox communist regime. Bulgaria has traditional links with Europe and it was a market economy and democracy in the period between the two world wars. This gives hope for more radical changes and even for the election of a non-communist government in the early 1990s. There is a potential for such developments.

Problems of the economic reforms

Most of the Eastern European economies have embarked on a road which no one has travelled before: the attempt to liberalise, or turn into a free market, a command planned economy. Neither theory nor the experience of previous reforms suggest clearly what would be the optimal strategy for achieving these goals or what are the best answers to such questions as: what is the right proportion between public and market goods, between state administration and market, or between achieving capital profitability and welfare goals. The present economic reforms in Eastern Europe have many problems which I will briefly discuss here. The progress of reform is painfully slow and accompanied by contradictions in government policies, miscalculations and mistakes in all of these countries. In some of the CMEA countries (Poland, Hungary) the reform is carried out in a (collapsing) economy which is in a crisis situation (huge domestic and external imbalances). The main problems of the reform are the following:

  huge domestic budget deficits and monetary overhang (except in Czechoslovakia) and inflationary pressure;
  large external debt and shortage of foreign currency;
  bad luck from external disturbances: falling oil, gas and coal prices in late 1980s, Czernobyl and Armenia disasters, burden of the Afghanistan war, bad harvest in 1988;

measures to affect the power of the bureaucracy are still not effective
and the autonomy of the enterprises is in reality illusionary;

ambiguous attitudes towards private, cooperative and concessionaire businesses which in some countries (Soviet Union,
Czechoslovakia) are regarded by certain groups as a 'threat to
socialism' and as 'creating classes';

shortages in agriculture – food shortages, losses (waste) in grain
production and others;[8]

labour unrest: pressure for wage inflation and new willingness to
strike (Czechoslovakia, Bulgaria, Romania, GDR);

national unrest: independence movements and ethnic tensions in
the Soviet Union (Baltic republics, Armenia, Azerbaidjan),
Bulgaria, Hungary, Romania;

problems arising from the underdeveloped forms of economic
cooperation within the CMEA area – 'barter-type' trade,
pressures to change the price system etc.;

corruption in the trade system (shops, restaurants, etc.);

the inability of a large number of the decision makers to adjust to the
requirements of the *perestroika* system and the new situation;

resistance to change from the bureaucracy, working class, etc., and
lack of private initiative and risk taking

Many observers agree that economic reform in the Soviet Union has
still not taken off. 'Barter-type' relations developed among domestic
enterprises.

According to the Soviet academician Aganbegyan the most crucial
difficulty in the Soviet Union at present is the budget deficit. He stated
that the deficit exceeded 120 billion roubles ($US 190 billion) in 1989
(*The Financial Times*, 3 October 1989, p. 2). The main reasons for the
huge budget deficit are: falling oil and gas export prices, increased
subsidies for agriculture, reduced revenues from sales of vodka.
Another problem is the unregulated money supply. Inflation is high in
Poland (hyperinflation up to 1,000 per cent in 1989) and Hungary
(more than 40 per cent), and is increasing in the Soviet Union (more
than 9 per cent). Price reform in the Soviet Union was postponed
because of fear of inflation and according to the Soviet Professor L.
Abalkin 'because of the faltering state of the economy' (*The Financial
Times*, 2 December 1988, p. 2).[9] In some of the other Eastern European
countries (e.g. Czechoslovakia) there is a 'great deal of scepticism'
about the prospects of successful economic reform. A Czechoslovak
scholar stated that 'faith in the possible success of reform strivings is
now significantly smaller than it was twenty years ago, both among

Table 1. *Economic reform 1989*

	Command economy	*State pre-emption*	*Market systems*
Industry	Romania GDR	Soviet Union Czechoslovakia	Poland Bulgaria Hungary
Agriculture	*State farming* Romania	*Collectives/ procurement* Soviet Union Czechoslovakia GDR	*Decollectivisation* Bulgaria Hungary Poland
Foreign Trade	*Central control* Romania	*Decentralisation* Czechoslovakia, GDR, Poland, Bulgaria	*Direct trade abroad* Hungary Soviet Union

citizens and in the leadership'.[10] The new Czechoslovak leadership, however, will probably suggest a strategy for a gradual market orientation of the economy. A research project carried out under the guidance of the prominent Hungarian and Harvard Professor J. Kornai came to the conclusion that despite several years of economic reform (beginning in 1968) in Hungary, the following main problems existed in the economy in the early 1980s:[11]

1 a huge proportion of fiscal profit redistribution;
2 almost complete separation of original profit and final profit;
3 levelling to a low profit level;
4 weak (or perverse) relation between profit and investment;
5 no connection between wages and profit rate;
6 preference given to large enterprises.[12]

Economic reform: summary

The main conclusions of the above discussion on the state of economic reforms in Eastern Europe in the late 1980s are summarised in table 1.

The state of economic reform in Eastern Europe is characterised by three main developments. Firstly, departure from a command economic system and market-oriented structural changes in industry.

Secondly, collectives play an important role in agriculture but the trend towards decollectivisation is strong. Thirdly, decentralisation of the system of foreign economic relations and direct trade abroad.

In some of the Eastern European countries, for example, Poland and Hungary, economic plans of late 1989 suggest that efforts are being directed towards radical changes and the creation of a free-market economy in the 1990s. In the Soviet Union the trend towards decentralisation and increasing the role of the market signals in the allocation of resources is strong. Bulgaria's reform demonstrates an attempt at a departure from policies maintaining the 'happy' stagnation of the 1970s and 1980s but new reforms (e.g. ownership reform, tax reform, and others) are needed in order to prepare the economy for radical market-oriented changes. Its probable membership in the IMF and the World Bank will encourage such a development. Czechoslovakia's reform in the late 1980s is less advanced than other Eastern European countries; it was more an effort of the bureaucracy to reform itself than a decisive break with the centrally planned economy as in Poland, Hungary, the Soviet Union and Bulgaria.

Political reform and social changes

As mentioned earlier, the present economic reforms in the Eastern European countries and particularly in Poland, Hungary, Bulgaria, Czechoslovakia and the Soviet Union are accompanied by substantial attempts at *political reform*. It is clearly seen that the changes envisaged by economic reform would not 'work' without the advancement of political reform. The Soviet Union's political reform agenda is *perestroika* (restructuring), *glasnost*, *democratizatsiya* (democratisation), and (in the Soviet context of socialist) pluralism. It is envisaged that a transfer of all the party's economic managerial functions, both local and central, to the government (Soviets), should occur rapidly, as well as setting a limit of two five-year terms for holders of elected offices both in the party and in the government. A new Soviet parliament was elected in March 1989 which will meet for longer periods during the year, and the election of an executive style president is based more on the French than on the United States model. Opposition groups (in the Soviet Union and Czechoslovakia) and opposition parties (in Poland, Hungary, Bulgaria, Romania) are increasing their activity and influence in the parliaments (the influence of groups is, however, still less relevant for Romania) and in the case of Poland, Czechoslovakia and Hungary in the government.

This brief discussion points out that for the first time in more than seventy years of Soviet history changes in the political life are planned. However, it will take time to see the results in real life.[13] The political changes in Poland, Hungary, Czechoslovakia and Bulgaria will be much more advanced.

The social changes as a result of *perestroika* at present are a transformation in the relations between 'rulers' and 'ruled'. However, positive support for *perestroika* comes from only 15 per cent of the Soviet population (mainly the 'intelligentsia'). The surprisingly announced referendum in the Soviet Union in the second half of 1990 for the market-oriented changes in the economy was an effort to increase public support for the unpopular measures of the Gorbachev leadership (rising prices, danger of unemployment). However, interviews in the Soviet Union and in the other East European countries suggest that the greater part of the population does not know what a 'market' is, or 'market-oriented' changes in the economy. Y. S. Shatalin, an economic advisor to Gorbachev, stated in early 1990 that if you ask them (the Soviet people) do they want a market, they will say 'no', and 'no, again'. So the question must be very 'precise' (*The Financial Times*, 29 May 1990, p. 1). There is a strongly hostile attitude towards private businesses and prejudice against the cooperative movement. There were reports that the activities of cooperatives in the Soviet Union were criticised even in the parliament (*The Financial Times*, 27 September 1989, p. 2). There is growing concern in Hungary that some self-managed firms are selling their property at unreasonably low prices to foreign investors.

East–West relations

Perestroika has an important impact on developments in East–West relations. The Soviet foreign minister dismissed in a speech in 1988 the 'class basis' of international relations, which was one of the main ideological pillars of Soviet diplomacy in the past. Gorbachev's speech to the United Nations in December 1988 underlined the message of 'new thinking' in Soviet foreign policy. Progress was achieved in the East–West dialogue on the Soviet involvement in Afghanistan, the Helsinki Review Meeting in Vienna on human rights in the Soviet Union and Eastern Europe, the talks on conventional armed forces and security-building measures in Europe and others. A historic Sino-Soviet summit took place in 1989. Soviet diplomacy is showing a new dynamism in bilateral contacts with the United States, the United Kingdom, France, Italy and West Germany and is recognising the significance of the European Community as an interlocutor. The individual Eastern European countries have completed bilateral negotiations on new trade accords with the European Community. Hungary went further and discussed the possibility of an affiliation to the European Community while remaining in the CMEA during a visit to Strasbourg by a Hungarian delegation (*The Financial Times*, 28 February 1989, p. 2). Poland is also considering such an affiliation. Hungary and Poland are also increasingly interested in joining the European Free Trade Association (EFTA). An association with the European Community is considered also by some other East European countries (Bulgaria, Czechoslovakia). Hungary, Czechoslovakia and Poland demonstrated in early 1990 their willingness to develop regional cooperation with Austria and some other Western European countries (e.g. Italy) as part of a strategy for (re)integration into Europe.

The present Soviet approach to the Far East and to the Asia-Pacific region is pragmatic in the light of the economic development of the Soviet territories in the Far East. Soviet foreign policy is showing a new dynamism in relations with the Arab countries (and particularly the Middle East), and with Latin America and Africa.

The Soviet and the American leaders realise that each superpower cannot achieve strategic superiority over the other. While in the 1970s and early 1980s national security concerns in both countries were given priority over economic matters, in the late 1980s and probably in the 1990s the primacy of economic concerns will be established. There is a movement away from the spirit of ideological crusade in the Soviet Union and in the United States. Both countries, and their allies, are starting to re-evaluate old international commitments in the light of new economic, political and military realities. The Soviet leader appealed in a letter to the meeting of the heads of the seven leading industrialised countries in Paris in July 1989 for global cooperation in economic matters and asked that the Soviet Union should also participate in the coordination of macroeconomic policies of the Group of Seven. Hungary actively supported the emigration of many thousands of citizens of the German Democratic Republic to West Germany in 1989 and some reformers in Hungary are voicing the idea of Hungarian political neutrality in ten or fifteen years (*The Financial Times*, 6 October 1989, p. 2). In the USA, Henry Kissinger proposed in early 1989 a plan for a 'Second Yalta', dealing with the influence of the Soviet Union and the USA in Eastern Europe (*The Financial Times*, 29 March 1989, p. 9).

However, there are some differences in the individual Western countries' attitudes towards the Soviet Union's and Eastern Europe's *perestroika* policy. On the one hand, the United Kingdom and the United States regarded 'developments so far' in Eastern Europe as positive, but suggest 'a wait-and-see attitude by the West' in the late 1980s. On the other hand, as discussed in the EC foreign ministers meeting in October 1988, and in subsequent meetings, West Germany and Italy argued that the changes set in motion by Gorbachev 'serve Western interests and deserve immediate support' (*The Financial Times*, 17 October 1988, p. 4). The British foreign minister, Sir Geoffrey Howe, stressed that the West should not overestimate its capacity to influence Soviet reforms and that Western policy should be 'No Marshall Plans, no gratuitous concessions'. He argued further that Western economic assistance cannot substitute for thoroughgoing and permanent reform of the Soviet economy.[14] The West German minister for economic affairs stated that the West can help the reforming Eastern European countries 'only indirectly, by helping them to help themselves' (*The Financial Times*, 17 October 1989, p. 2). The West German minister of foreign affairs, Genscher, stressed in an interview in February 1990 that the FRG will support the East European needs for stable partnership with the West (*Stabilitätspartnerschaft*), new disarmament policy, financial help and new loans. The present Western attitude towards doing business with Eastern Europe is that economic cooperation should be based on commercial calculations of mutual advantage and trade and that more joint ventures should be promoted, the provision of suitable credits providing encouragement. However, in the case of Poland and Hungary where developments towards radical political and economic changes were much advanced in late 1989, the USA, Canada, Japan, the European Community and Switzerland took steps to provide aid packages to both countries. The Western countries aim, at some point, to coordinate their efforts to support the reforming movements in Eastern Europe and particularly in Poland, Hungary and Czechoslovakia. The continuity of aid to Poland and Hungary would be very important. An important issue in this context is how much aid should be provided, and what its timing should be. The changes in Bulgaria, Czechoslovakia and the GDR in late 1989 led to a reconsideration of Western economic policies towards Eastern Europe. The decision to establish a European Bank for Reconstruction and Development is a step towards closer cooperation with this region. All of this indicates that there is a good chance that the late 1980s and the 1990s 'detente' holds the promise of being deeper and much longer lasting than the 1970s 'detente'.

Reforming foreign trade mechanism

Some of the major changes in the Eastern European foreign trade mechanism were mentioned in the previous section. I will discuss briefly here the main directions of foreign trade reform in the Soviet Union; the reforms in the individual Eastern European countries resemble to a great extent the Soviet model.[15]

The foreign trade reforms were announced in August 1986 and came into effect from 1 January 1987. In a presentation for Ambrosetti to British businessmen, academician Aganbegyan, an economic advisor to Gorbachev, stated that the Soviet Union had abandoned the Stalinist state monopoly of foreign trade. The right of trading abroad had been given to twenty ministries, whereas previously it was the monopoly of the Foreign Trade Ministry. More than seventy domestic firms now had the right to make direct contacts with the international markets: some 1,000 firms had the right to make direct contacts with CMEA enterprises. After 1 April 1989 all enterprises, associations, cooperatives and other organisations whose products (work, services) are competitive on the foreign market are allowed to carry out direct export-import operations (*Foreign Trade*, Moscow, no 2, 1989, pp. 44–9). Convertibility of the rouble is planned by the late 1990s. There are discussions on the establishment of a Soviet export credit agency (*The Financial Times*, 28 October 1988, p. 5). Hard currency auctions have operated from late 1989.

All this indicates that the foreign trade reform is focused firstly on rationalising the administrative and planning structure, and secondly, on decentralisation of foreign trade decision making from the centre to the enterprises. The chairman of the State Foreign Economic Commission stated that the 'implementation of state foreign trade monopoly in its general state aspects remains centralised, with its current functions being gradually passed down to the level of economic entities'.[16] The organisational structure of the Soviet foreign trade system is presented in Figure 1.

According to the chairman of the Soviet Chamber of Commerce and Industry the main directions of the ongoing foreign trade reforms are decentralisation of external economic ties, diversification of the forms of economic cooperation (more joint ventures), harmonisation of domestic and world prices, creation of effective foreign trade policy

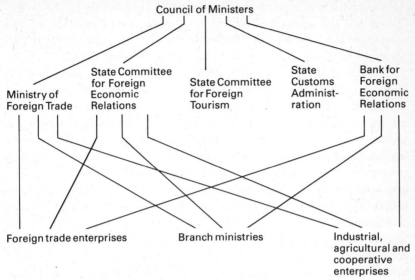

Figure 1 The Soviet foreign trade system

instruments (new legislation and customs tariffs, revision of non-tariff regulations, import and export licensing, adoption of a new system of commodity description and coding, etc.), activating the relations with GATT, the European Community, and The European Free Trade Association.[17] There is strong Soviet interest in applying for membership in the IMF and the World Bank.

From January 1988 the Soviet banking system was reorganised on sectoral specialisation principles: in addition to the State Bank, five banks relating to specific sectors of industry with branches in the individual Soviet republics were created for direct on-site service to companies and customers. The envisaged changes affect first of all the domestic sphere, although many of them extend also to foreign economic activities.[18]

There are changes in the banking system in the other Eastern European countries. In Bulgaria the Bank for Economic Projects and eight other banks were created which have the right to use foreign credit. The Polish Export Development Bank started operations in 1987. In Hungary international operations are conducted by specialised credit institutions and by mixed and foreign banks. That indicates that in Hungary and in Bulgaria foreign exchange can be borrowed not only by the central and foreign trade banks but also by other credit agencies.

Two of the major goals of the foreign trade reforms in the Soviet Union are the convertibility of the rouble and a realistic rouble exchange rate. In 1988 a Politburo plan was announced for full convertibility up to the year 2000 (*The Financial Times*, 10 October 1988, p. 1). The chairman of the CMEA International Investment Bank stated in 1989 that the issue of convertibility had been seriously discussed by the CMEA countries and one might expect that they will introduce a convertibility of their national currencies within CMEA up to the mid-1990s (IMF *Morning Press*, 18 October 1989). At the 43rd CMEA Council Session in 1987, the Soviet prime minister made a proposal for limited financial convertibility which envisaged, firstly, application only to CMEA transactions, secondly, gradual implementation over ten years, and thirdly, application initially only to selected merchandise deals, e.g., for goods traded between CMEA firms having direct production relations with each other. The proposal was accepted only by Bulgaria and Czechoslovakia. (It should be mentioned here, however, that the measures which some of the CMEA countries – the GDR, Hungary – introduced in 1988–9 to restrict exports of consumer goods were adverse to the idea of transferability and convertibility within the CMEA area.)

Academician Aganbegyan wrote that one of the most frequent questions he has had to answer in many discussions in the Soviet Union and abroad is will the rouble become convertible, and if so, when? (Aganbegyan, 1989, p. 209). He expects that rouble convertibility will be introduced in the next seven to ten years in stages: first, domestic convertibility (*commodity* convertibility – goods may be bought freely by domestic residents, or in other words money provides unconditional access to goods, including means of production, consumer goods like housing, cars and others – and some kind of internal *currency* convertibility, meaning businesses and individuals may buy foreign currency freely on a domestic currency market), followed by convertibility with the CMEA countries (and with the transferable rouble, the CMEA international currency), and the third stage will be convertibility with all other countries (Aganbegyan, 1988b, p. 41). He stressed also that there were considerations to create either a second currency, a 'hard rouble' backed by a combination of gold and foreign currency reserves and by exports, or a 'parallel rouble' devoted entirely to foreign trade and capital transactions (sort of 'chervonets' currency during NEP in the 1920s): all these changes should be preceded by price reform. Other Soviet economists (e.g. Anikin, 1989; Doronin, 1988; Kuznetsov, 1988) suggest the establishment of an exchange market restricted to residents. Anikin (1989, p. 3) argues that 'if any real form of convertibility is introduced it can only function under the system of more or less stable exchange rates. To ensure this relative stability the state will have to effect regulation and market intervention which presupposes existence of sufficient foreign exchange reserves and/or access to money markets, including probably the support on the part of the IMF.' In a recently published article, Konstantinov (1989) argues that the currency convertibility is an 'objective necessity' at present (p. 35), but it should be introduced gradually (p. 33). In principle, his plan resembles the Aganbegyan proposal. There are proposals from Soviet economists (Petrakov) for introduction of a realistic exchange rate before price reforms (in contrast to Aganbegyan and Konstantinov). In connection with the Soviet proposals for the existence of an official and a parallel currency it has to be mentioned here, however, that the convertibility of one of these currencies at present would not have the same effect on the Soviet (non-market) economy as the 'chervonets' in the 1920s, in a time when there was, for example, a gold exchange standard and controls on foreign exchange operations were very strict. The 'parallel rouble' might be applied first in the Soviet so-called 'special economic zones' for activating relations with foreign investors and firms (Soviet–Finnish border, Far East region) (*The Financial Times*, 4 April 1989, p. 2). In the presence of huge domestic monetary overhang (households and enterprises) its existence, however, will affect rapid devaluation of the official currency.

There are plans for a further 100 per cent devaluation of the rouble by January 1991 which will apply to purchases of convertible currency by Soviet enterprises and plans for the abolition of the use of some 3,000 foreign currency coefficients covering different products in exchange with different countries in favour of one rate. It should be mentioned here, however, that a devaluation of the rouble was initially planned for January 1990. The successful implementation of these plans depends, of course, on the successful and simultaneous introduction of the economic reform. The price reform is very important in this respect. But, as was mentioned earlier, the price reform has been postponed. However, one might argue that the approach first to introduce a meaningful unified exchange rate and then to gradually correct domestic prices by linking them to foreign prices, as in the case of Hungary and Poland, could also create the conditions for the convertibility of the rouble. But the most important condition for introducing convertibility of the rouble and convertibility of the other Eastern European currencies is the existence of real markets in these countries. The convertibility is not a pre-condition for creating a market, but a consequence of it. And convertibility *per se* will not resolve the economic problems of the Eastern European countries at present. The non-convertibility (commodity and currency) in the centrally planned economies in Eastern Europe in the 1950s to 1980s has been a result of the central planning and allocation of resources, leading to a 'shortage' economy. Convertibility and central planning are incompatible. Radical market-oriented economic reform is the only answer to the question of how to approach the issue of convertibility. Creating a multilateral clearing union, with the participation of the Eastern European and some of the Western countries (e.g. from the European Community) and similar to the clearing union established in the 1950s in Western Europe – the European Payments Union – with American help, could provide the grounds for promoting multilateralism, and transferability and consequently lead gradually to currency convertibility in Eastern Europe. Such a scenario requires, of course, specific political conditions in both the East and the West. In a market economy there are two main factors for the convertibility of an overvalued currency (as in the case of the Eastern European currencies): currency devaluations and tight monetary policies. However, without going into details it is worth mentioning here that in the transition from central planning to market the modified planned economies (in other words, economies introducing market-oriented changes) tend to have a 'perverse' response to devaluation, in the sense of devaluation causing a deterioration in the hard-currency trade balance and a widening of the external disequilibrium (Wolf, 1988, p. 60).

The above discussion indicates that radical market-oriented reform (and their successful implementation) of the price, exchange rate, monetary and fiscal policies, and market-oriented institutional changes in the financial and banking system (competing banks, stock exchange, etc.) are the only 'road' to convertibility of the national currencies of the Eastern European countries. Poland is introducing such reforms from 1 January 1990. It is hard to say whether the existing convertible currency auctions are an embryonic form of a domestic convertibility. But there is no doubt that they are a step in that direction. There is a type of very limited convertibility of the national CMEA currencies for non-commercial payments (tourism) within the CMEA as well as the CMEA joint investment currency coefficients, and the currency coefficients between the Soviet rouble and the TR.

This all indicates that the main problems in reforming the foreign trade system in Eastern Europe as a region – rational price system, realistic exchange rate and convertibility – will not be soon solved.

Capital markets in Eastern Europe

The economic reforms in Eastern Europe envisage liberalisation of product and labour markets. The creation of some sort of 'socialist market economy' raises the importance of the discipline of the market which cannot be achieved without capital markets. Monetary and financial reform in Eastern Europe is a compelling logical sequence in the implementation of economic reform. The creation of limited markets for products leads to arguments for escalation in favour of labour and capital markets. This bears out Maurice Dobb's statement that elements of different economic systems (e.g. centrally planned and market economies) cannot be mixed in just any proportions, as can be done with a cake, varying ingredients to taste (cited in Nuti, 1989, p. 434).

At present Poland, Hungary, Bulgaria and the Soviet Union among the Eastern European countries have been cautious in developing capital markets and breaking with the 'documonetary' regulations of the economy.[19] As discussed above banking reforms were introduced in 1987–8. In Hungary central banking has been separated from commercial banking for the first time in 1987. The Central Bank exercises monetary policy (reserve and liquidity ratios, rediscounting rates, issuing of securities etc.) while the commercial banks provide credits on the basis of the enterprises' creditworthiness. The goal is for budgetary grants and 'documonetary' relations to be replaced by contractual relations with the banks. Bulgaria, Poland and the Soviet Union adopted the Hungarian model banking reform. The Soviet Union's plans are for the central bank to be a 'blend of the US Federal Reserve System and the Bank of England', according to the Soviet ambassador to the European Community (IMF, *Morning Press*, 20 October 1989).

Bonds, shares, and foreign exchange auctions are part of the policy to activate market guided relations among enterprises in Eastern Europe. They are the first steps towards the creation of capital markets. Some sort of bond market has operated in Hungary since 1983: primary issues and secondary trading for enterprises and households. Shares were also issued and traded only within state firms until 1988. However, from January 1989 equity market operations are extended also to households. Hungary was the first Eastern European country to launch a share issue on the Western market: Novotrade, a software and computer company placed an issue in 1989 (*The Economist*, 21 October 1989, p. 79). The Hungarian reform envisages further steps activating the role of the insurance companies and pension funds on the market. In Poland the first treasury bills worth £330 million were issued in 1989 (IMF, *Morning Press*, 3 October 1989).

In the Soviet Union state firms and cooperatives are allowed to issue shares, however, only employees of the enterprises are allowed to buy shares. There are plans to make 'enterprise shares' available for other state and cooperative firms. Money raised by the share sales should be fully invested in production.[20] There are in the Soviet Union a few agencies which finance export promotion and domestic ventures, and which are allowed to issue bonds and accept deposits in foreign currencies and roubles. Eurocard and Mastercard signed an agreement with the Soviet Union in 1988 and Soviet savings banks are considering issuing credit cards on their own account.

Foreign exchange auctions have been organised in Poland (since autumn 1987) through the Export Development Bank, as well as in Bulgaria, the Soviet Union and Czechoslovakia. In Poland the convertible currency sales on auctions are expected to increase further in 1989–90 due to an increase in currency supply coming from holders of export revenue accounts (*Rzeczpospolita*, no. 265, 15 November 1988). In Bulgaria the auction price for foreign exchange is almost 7.5 times higher than the official rates.

The above discussion points to the conclusion that there are embryonic forms of capital markets in some of the Eastern European countries. However, these countries still do not have a blueprint for developing their domestic capital markets (stock markets, bond markets, different financial institutions) and opening them to foreign participation. In 1989 Poland discussed several schemes for privatisation, including a programme for the establishment of investment and commercial banks initially being state owned and later operating as joint holding companies (*The Financial Times*, 'East European Markets', 22 September 1989, p. 2). The opening of the domestic capital markets would imply that external disturbances and international share price movements will be transmitted to the economy through these markets. To the knowledge of the author there are no studies in Eastern Europe, or in the West, on the question of what would be the effect of such developments on the domestic economies, and particularly on the economies of the highly indebted countries.

Some of the main problems connected with the creation of capital markets in Eastern Europe are: firstly, lack of financial discipline (huge budget deficits, monetary overhang, fiscal profit redistribution); secondly, vast excess demand totally incompatible with a successful implementation of monetary and financial reform; thirdly, lack of market clearing prices and convertibility; and fourthly, lack of efficient decentralisation of economic decision making, since monetary reforms require such a decentralisation.

2 The Eastern European external debt situation

The accumulation of the Eastern European convertible-currency debt continued in the second half of the 1980s. Poland and Hungary remained the most indebted CMEA countries and two of the most indebted among the developing countries. The Soviet Union increased its borrowing on the international capital markets. Bulgaria's external disequilibrium rapidly rose during 1987–8, in contrast with its previous conservative borrowing policies. The Eastern European region's debt which in the early 1980s marked the beginning of the international debt crisis is still considered to be of certain concern for the international financial markets. This chapter attempts to discuss the question as to whether the convertible currency debt servicing difficulties were (and are) inherent in the economic development of Eastern Europe in the late 1980s.

Is there a region-wide debt problem in Eastern Europe?

In order to answer this question[1] an analysis is required of the main developments[2] in the balance of trade, the current account, capital flows, terms of borrowing, and the main indicators of the debt burden and creditworthiness since the beginning of the 1980s.[3]

Trade balances. In 1983–7 the aggregate visible trade balance (Table 2) of the Eastern European countries was positive but was negative with market economies in 1986–7 due to increased imports (Bulgaria, Czechoslovakia, GDR, Hungary) from the West (Table 3) and the deterioration of the terms of trade (Table 4). Hungary, the Soviet Union and Bulgaria ran the biggest trade deficits with developed market economies in 1985–7 (Table 2). Romania continued its policy of restricting imports, reducing them from the West by 30 per cent in 1987 (Table 3).

Current accounts. The Soviet Union and the Eastern European Six

Table 2. *CMEA current account balances with market economies*
1980–1987
(billions of US dollars)

	Total	Trade of which developed market economies	Net services plus transfers Total	Investment income	Current account
Bulgaria					
1980	1.0	0.1	−0.1	−0.4	1.0
1983	0.4	−0.3		−0.2	0.4
1985	−0.3	−0.6	0.2	−0.1	−0.3
1986	−0.9	−1.5	−0.1	−0.3	−0.9
1987	0.4	−0.8		−0.3	0.4
Czechoslovakia					
1980	0.1	−0.4	−0.4	−0.3	−0.4
1983	0.8	0.1	−0.3	−0.3	0.5
1985	0.6	0.2	−0.06	0.1	0.5
1986	0.4	−0.1	−0.2	−0.2	0.2
1987	−0.2	−0.8	−0.2	−0.2	−0.4
GDR					
1980	−1.7	−1.7	−0.1	−1.2	−1.8
1983	1.4	1.0	0.3	−1.0	1.7
1985	0.9	0.7	0.1	−0.6	1.0
1986	0.5	0.3	0.8	−0.8	1.3
1987	−0.2	−0.7	1.1	−0.8	0.9
Hungary					
1980	−0.7	−0.6	−0.6	−0.4	−1.3
1983	−0.1		−0.6	−0.7	−0.6
1985	0.2	−0.5	−0.49	−0.56	0.03
1986	−0.5	−0.7	−0.9	−0.8	−1.4
1987	−0.3	−0.7	−0.7	−0.9	−1.0
Poland					
1980	−1.0	−0.7	−1.8	−2.3	−2.8
1983	1.4	0.9	−2.3	−2.7	−0.9
1985	1.0	0.6	−1.8	−2.5	−0.7
1986	0.9	0.5	−1.2	−2.6	−0.3
1987	1.0	1.0	−1.3	−2.8	−0.3

Table 2 (*cont.*)

Romania					
1980	− 1.9		− 0.9	− 0.8	− 2.8
1983	1.6	2.3	− 0.8	− 0.7	0.8
1985	2.0	2.55	− 0.54	− 0.54	1.5
1986	1.9	2.2	− 0.5	− 0.6	1.4
1987	2.0	2.5	− 0.3	− 0.4	1.7
Eastern Europe Six					
1980	− 4.2	− 3.2	− 3.9	− 5.4	− 8.1
1983	5.5	3.9	− 3.6	− 5.5	1.9
1985	4.4	3.0	− 2.6	− 4.2	2.0
1986	2.3	0.6	− 2.1	− 5.3	0.2
1987	2.8	0.5	− 1.5	− 5.4	1.3
Soviet Union					
1980	3.4	2.4	0.2	− 1.2	3.6
1983	6.2	2.5	− 0.1	− 1.4	6.1
1985	0.7	− 0.6	− 0.1	0.2	0.6
1986	1.4	− 4.3	− 0.5	− 1.7	0.9
1987	8.0	− 0.7	− 0.5	− 1.7	7.5
Total					
1980	− 0.8	− 0.8	− 4.3	− 7.1	− 5.0
1983	11.8	6.5	− 4.0	− 7.2	7.7
1985	5.1	2.4	− 2.7	− 4.0	2.6
1986	3.8	− 3.7	− 2.8	− 7.3	0.9
1987	10.7	− 0.2	− 2.3	− 7.3	8.5

Source: Zloch-Christy (1988), pp. 43–5; United Nations Economic Commission for Europe, 'Recent Changes in Europe's Trade', *Economic Bulletin for Europe*, 1988, p. 742.

increased their total current account surplus from $US 2.6 billion in 1985 and $US 0.9 billion in 1986 to $8.5 billion in 1987 (Table 2), due mostly to trade surpluses with the developing market economies. Poland ran deficits for the whole of 1980–7; Hungary's current account remained negative in 1980–3 and 1986–7; Bulgaria and Czechoslovakia experienced deterioration of their current accounts in 1985–6 and 1987 respectively. The Soviet Union, Romania and the GDR had positive current accounts in 1982–7.

Gross and net debt. The gross and net debt of the Eastern European countries after a 'stabilization' period in 1982–4 increased again in the following years (Tables 5 and 6). The total gross and net debt grew in

Table 3. *Annual changes in value of East–West trade, 1983–1987*
(percentages)

	Eastern European exports					Eastern European imports				
	1983	1984	1985	1986	1987	1983	1984	1985	1986	1987
Bulgaria	− 12	3	− 2	10	16	2	− 6	26	17	− 9
Czecho-slovakia		3	− 5	14	16	− 8	− 5	8	19	29
GDR		− 2	− 3	14	9	7	− 13	2	26	24
Hungary	3	9	2	13	20	− 9	− 3	11	21	9
Poland		19	1	5	11	− 8	4	7	7	18
Romania	7	34	− 6	4	− 2	− 23	6	4	17	− 30
Eastern Europe Six	1	10	− 2	10	10	− 5	− 5	8	18	11
Soviet Union	− 2	3	− 11	− 11	1	− 4	− 2	− 1	− 3	− 3
Total	− 1	6	− 8	− 2	6	− 4	− 3	2	6	4

Source: United Nations Economic Commission for Europe, 'Recent Changes in Europe's Trade', *Economic Bulletin for Europe*, 1988, p. 745.

Table 4. *Changes in terms of trade in East–West trade, 1983–1987*
(Index 1975 = 100)

	1983	1984	1985	1986	1987[a]
Eastern Europe	152	154	147	109	96
Eastern Europe Six	114	114	110	100	96
Soviet Union	189	200	192	118	96

[a] estimates
Source: United Nations, *Economic Bulletin for Europe*, 1988, p. 743.

1987 by 13 per cent and 19 per cent respectively. The total gross debt amounted to $128.6 billion (excluding CMEA banks) and $129.1 billion in 1987 and 1988 respectively. The net debt reached $99.45 billion in 1987; its level was $73.7 billion (including CMEA banks) in the crisis year 1981. In 1988 the net debt was slightly reduced to $97.25 billion. The debt of Hungary and the Soviet Union grew particularly fast: the Soviet net debt rose by 35 per cent in 1987 in comparison to 1986 and remained more than $23 billion in 1988. Bulgaria and Czechoslovakia also increased their borrowing and hence raised their liabilities

Table 5. *Eastern European convertible-currency gross debt 1980–1988* *(millions of US dollars, end-period)*

	1980	1981	1982	1983	1984	1985	1986	1987	1988
Bulgaria	3,560	3,060	2,760	2,610	2,300	2,409	5,075	6,000	7,300
Czecho-slovakia	4,930	4,500	4,050	3,700	3,350	3,013	4,254	5,300	5,700
GDR	14,100	14,900	13,000	12,650	12,880	13,108	15,764[a]	18,500[a]	20,000[a]
Hungary	9,090	8,699	7,715	8,250	8,900	11,260	15,086	17,500	16,800
Romania	9,557	10,160	9,766	8,880	7,480	6,000	6,395	5,700	4,000
CMEA 5	41,227	41,309	37,281	36,090	34,910	35,790	46,574	53,000	53,800
Poland	25,000	26,411	26,975	26,396	26,980	30,204	33,526	37,600	37,300
CMEA 6	66,227	67,720	64,256	64,486	61,890	65,994	80,100	90,600	91,100
Soviet Union	17,800	20,900	20,000	20,500	21,600	25,193	33,061[b]	38,000[b]	38,000[b]
CMEA banks	4,650	4,250	3,800	3,600	3,600	2,500	na	na	na
Total	88,677	92,870	88,056	86,586	87,090	93,687	113,161	128,600	129,100

[a] Includes debt to FRG
[b] Includes CMEA banks
Source: Zloch-Christy (1988), p. 50; OECD, 'East–West financial relations: recent developments and medium-term prospects', in *Financial Market Trends*, no. 39, Paris, 1988, p. 24, OECD, 'East–West trade and financial relations: developments in 1987–1988 and Future prospects'. *Financial Market Trends*, no. 42, Paris, 1989, p. 24.

towards Western commercial bank creditors. The gross and net debt of Bulgaria grew particularly rapidly in 1986–8; net debt increased by more than 73 per cent in 1987–8. Romania was the only Eastern European country which rigorously reduced gross and net debt in 1982–8. Poland remained the most indebted CMEA country with an estimated $35.3 billion and $34.0 billion net debt in 1987 and 1988 respectively (Table 6).

New credits. The Eastern European countries (except Romania and Poland) increased their borrowing from commercial banks in the period 1984–8. The total of CMEA liabilities rose by $5.6 billion and $3.9 billion in 1985 and 1986 respectively. The Eastern European countries continued to build up their reserves with BIS banks in 1983–5, but in 1986–7 they considerably reduced their assets, particularly the Soviet Union, Hungary and Bulgaria (Economic Commission for Europe, 1988, p. 758). The deterioration of their terms of trade and the falling revenues from exports of oil and gas were the

Table 6. *Eastern European convertible-currency net debt 1980–1988*
(millions of US dollars, end-period)

	1980	1981	1982	1983	1984	1985	1986	1987	1988
Bulgaria	2,771	2,220	1,736	1,501	850	635	3,694	4,600	6,400
Czecho slovakia	3,674	3,403	3,308	2,769	2,000	1,943	3,037	4,000	4,200
GDR	11,604	12,320	10,714	9,000	7,880	7,415	8,312[a]	10,500[a]	10,900[a]
Hungary	5,856	5,856	5,089	4,940	4,550	9,358	12,898	15,800	15,600
Romania	8,305	8,793	8,055	8,648	6,551	5,500	5,760	4,750	2,600
CMEA 5	32,210	32,592	28,902	24,858	21,831	24,851	33,701	39,650	39,700
Poland	23,646	24,663	25,725	25,253	24,115	28,606	31,805	35,300	34,050
CMEA 6	55,856	57,255	54,627	50,111	45,946	53,457	65,506	74,950	73,750
Soviet Union	9,628	12,520	9,896	10,783	10,493	14,545	18,292[b]	24,500[b]	23,500[b]
CMEA banks	4,250	3,950	3,550	3,350	3,300	2,500	na	na	na
Total	69,734	73,725	68,073	64,244	59,739	70,502	83,798	99,450	97,250

Source: see Table 5. *a* includes debt to FRG; *b* includes CMEA banks

main causes for these developments in the last two years of the period.

Table 7 shows the new funds raised by the CMEA countries on the international financial markets in the period 1980–8: they peaked at $5.2 billion in 1985 and remained high in 1986–8. Hungarian liabilities arose from what may be described best as 'overborrowing' and in addition to which there was an SDRs (Special Drawing Rights) 265 million stand-by credit from the IMF in May 1988 (*IMF Survey*, 17 October 1988, p. 333).

The Soviet Union also increased its borrowing, and in late 1987 placed its first foreign bond issue since 1917 – a Zurich flotation of 100 million Swiss francs – following this in July 1988 with a second bond issue in West Germany – D-Mark 500 million for 7 years, its $6\frac{3}{8}$ coupon being an interest rate cheaper than equivalent domestic borrowing by the German Federal Government (*The Financial Times*, 27 July 1988, p. 1). The third bond issue of D-Mark 750 million was placed in Germany in March 1989 (for 7 years and a 7 per cent coupon) (*The Financial Times*, 14 March 1989, p. 41). The Soviet Union borrowed more in 1988 than in any year since the mid-1970s. It received credits from Italy (the first governmental credit, $750 million, from any Western country since the Afghanistan invasion in 1979), West Germany (D-Mark 3 billion syndicated package), and France $2 billion syndicated bank package). There were negotiations to raise $1 billion from commercial banks in the United Kingdom in October 1988 (*The Financial Times*, 17 October 1988, p. 1).

Hungary continued her heavy borrowing in 1989. Some of the new credits she received included D-Mark 1 billion loan packages from Germany: DM500 million commercial bank credits guaranteed by the Federal government, and D-Mark 500 million commercial bank credits from the regional governments of Bavaria and Baden-Wuerttemberg (*The Financial Times*, 14 October 1989, p. 2). Poland received one of the first new loans after the debt crisis from the International Finance Corporation, affiliate of the IBRD (The World Bank) in 1988 ($16 million to encourage the growth of the private sector). As was mentioned earlier, in late 1989 aid packages including government guaranteed export credits were announced for Poland and Hungary. The approved (but not disbursed) loans were from the USA (some $837 million for Poland and $30 million for Hungary), Italy ($400 million), the European Investment Bank (for industrial projects and infrastructure) (*The Financial Times*, 20 October 1989, p. 1).

Borrowing terms. Table 8 shows the terms on syndicated Western bank credits to Eastern Europe measured in basis points over LIBOR in 1981–88. During 1982 to 1987 the CMEA countries as a group, and particularly the Soviet Union, borrowed at better terms than the general average rate and better also than developing countries not belonging to OPEC. The average margin for Eastern Europe fell to 24 base points in 1987, from a level of 112 basis points in 1983. In 1988 the margin increased to 30 basis points. Hungary was the only CMEA country which raised funds at a margin over 30 basis points in 1987, 1988 and 1989.

The *indicators of debt burden and creditworthiness* deteriorated in 1986–8 but still remained at tolerable levels for Eastern Europe as a region (Tables 9, 10 and 11). The debt service ratio (Table 9) in all these countries (except Czechoslovakia, the Soviet Union and Romania in 1988) was more than 30 per cent, a level which usually causes concern among bankers for future debt developments. Hungary's and Poland's debt service ratios were particularly high. The Bulgarian debt service ratio and the net debt/exports ratio (Table 10) deteriorated rapidly in 1986–88. Czechoslovakia's net debt/export ratio also deteriorated in 1986–88, reaching 81 per cent in 1987 from a level of 48 per cent in 1984–85 (Table 10). The liquidity ratios (Table 11) remained relatively stable in the period 1985–87 indicating the efforts being made by Eastern Europe to keep liquid assets at higher levels than at the

Table 7. Medium and long-term funds raised by Eastern European countries on the international financial markets, 1980–1988
(millions of US dollars)

	1980	1981	1982	1983	1984	1985	1986	1987	1988 Jan–June
Bulgaria	475					475	45	260	112
Czecho-slovakia	397	30	69	50		121	278	242	330
GDR	550	516	483	386	903	1,173	81	197	
Hungary	736	591		567	1,146	1,578	1,315	1,951	1,016
Poland	458				235				
Romania		337				150		30	
Eastern Europe Six	2,616	1,474	552	1,003	2,284	3,497	1,719	2,680	1,458
Soviet Union	50	25	153	68	867	1,489	1,821	1,003	2,644
CMEA banks		100			140	250	400	33	124
Total	2,666	1,600	704	1,071	3,291	5,236	3,940	3,716	4,226

Source: Zloch-Christy, 1988, p. 39; OECD, *Financial Market Trends*, no. 39, Paris, 1988, p. 33; Morgan Guaranty, *World Financial Markets*, 18 March 1988, p. 20, 9 September 1988, p. 18; OECD, *Financial Market Trends*, no. 42, Paris, 1989, p. 37.

Table 8. *Terms of syndicated credits to Eastern Europe, 1980–1988*

	1980	1981	1982	1983	1984	1985	1986	1987	1988
Eastern Europe Average Margin (*basis points over LIBOR*)	88	62	103	112	88	55	26	24	30
Eastern Europe Average Maturity (*years and months*)	6/7	5/7	4/9	4/5	5/11	7/5	7/5	8/3	8/5
OECD area (*basis points over LIBOR*)	na	58	56	65	55	41	36	28	
Other developing countries than OPEC (*basis points over LIBOR*)	na	104	114	170	144	99	67	60	
General average (*basis points over LIBOR*)	na	80	77	115	93	60	40	35	

Source: OECD, *Financial Market Trends*, no. 39, Paris, 1988, p. 33 and no. 42, 1989, p. 37; United Nations Economic Commission for Europe, *Economic Bulletin for Europe*, 1988, p. 761.

Table 9. *CMEA debt service ratios,[a] 1980–1988*

	1980	1981	1982	1983	1984	1985	1986	1987	1988
Bulgaria	35	33	34	29	16	14	31	30	36
Czecho-									
slovakia	24	19	18	22	25	31	17	18	16
GDR [b]	58	60	50	40	36	26	32	33	62
Hungary	25	40	36	34	50	70	61	47	52
Poland	99	87	80	68	70	109	61	71	68
Romania	27	38	41	42	15	26	29	32	22
Soviet									
Union	8	9	8	8	1	14	23	23	21

[a] All interest and amortization of medium- and long-term debt as a percentage of exports to market economies
[b] Excluding transactions with FRG
Source: Zloch-Christy (1988), pp. 64–5; OECD, *Financial Market Trends*, no. 39, 1988, Paris, p. 25–7; no. 42, 1989, p. 30.

Table 10. *CMEA net debt exports ratios, 1980–1988*

	1980	1981	1982	1983	1984	1985	1986	1987	1988
Bulgaria	91	88	80	52	27	20	142	149	184
Czecho-									
slovakia	81	84	79	66	49	48	67	81	80
GDR [a]	219	183	136	105	90	81	94	115	117
Hungary	118	120	102	99	93	210	287	297	274
Poland	299	427	489	428	385	474	489	465	431
Romania	126	121	129	106	58	80	100	83	39
Soviet									
Union	31	31	39	30	30	47	76	87	77

[a] Excluding transactions with FRG
Source: Zloch-Christy (1988), pp. 64–5; OECD, *Financial Market Trends*, no. 39, 1988, Paris, p. 25–7; no. 42, 1989, p. 29.

Table 11. *CMEA liquidity ratios, [a], 1980–1988*

	1980	1981	1982	1983	1984	1985	1986	1987	1988
Bulgaria	36	29	35	44	23	51	40	38	24
Czecho-slovakia	25	23	17	23	17	32	29	33	28
GDR	28	30	28	44	43	70	155	173	160
Hungary	29	19	16	30	35	44	45	30	24
Poland	8	13	24	30	17	32	32	51	49
Romania	3	4	6	12	8	10	13	31	31
Soviet Union	25	21	26	28	36	35	58	58	52

[a] Ratio of liquid assets to imports from market economies
Source: Zloch-Christy (1988), pp. 64–5; OECD, *Financial Market Trends*, no. 39, 1988, Paris, p. 25–7; no. 42, 1989, p. 31.

beginning of the 1980s, and particularly in the 'crisis years' 1981 and 1982. However, the liquidity ratios deteriorated in the Eastern Europe countries in 1988.

Author's estimates and some studies (Duwendag, 1987) suggest 'capital flight' problems in Eastern Europe, i.e. problems related to money 'fleeing' these countries as compared to 'normal' capital outflows for portfolio diversification abroad. Duwendag (1987, p. 14) points to some $3.0 billion (39 per cent of gross debt) and $3.4 billion (42 per cent of gross debt) in Hungary and Romania respectively in the period 1970–83. (One might speculate that such outflows from Poland in the same period were much larger.) Capital flight in Eastern Europe continued in the late 1980s, particularly in Hungary and Poland. In view of the exchange and capital controls (and restrictions) on private cross-border capital transactions in Eastern Europe one might suggest that government institutions were primarily involved in such transactions. Keeping part of foreign borrowings abroad appears to be the usual way. The black market for foreign currencies might be considered to be one of the vehicles used to transfer private funds abroad, particularly in the case of Hungary and Poland. The outflows of private funds from these countries increased greatly in late 1980s. However, no precise figures about orders of magnitude can be suggested because the analysis on 'capital flight' deals with admittedly enigmatic and incomplete statistical data.

This brief overflow of the balance of trade, flows of debt capital, terms of borrowing and the main indicators of the debt burden and creditworthiness points to the following conclusion. Eastern Europe as a region compared to Latin American and African countries effected an impressive adjustment[4] to its external convertible currency debt difficulties in the period 1982–85, using the traditional 'direct controls' of the centrally planned economies – changes in the allocation of resources among investment, government expenditure and exports; controls on the volume of imports; and controls on the supply of goods to households for consumption. The CMEA response to the debt shock in the early 1980s was a deflationary economic policy. The adjustment in Eastern Europe preceded the adjustment and forced austerity in Latin American debtor countries. The CMEA countries did not (or could not) rely on borrowing from the West to finance the trade and savings/investment gaps in 1981–83.

The indebtedness of Eastern Europe since 1985 is characterized by a continuing rise and by a deterioration of many debt-related indicators. The region as a whole, however, is still favourably viewed by the international financial markets but some hardening of lending conditions is visible (particularly for Hungary). There is a region-wide debt problem, but the debt situation has been manageable in the late 1980s. The debt difficulties of *Poland* are still those of insolvency leading to current and prospective inability to fulfil obligations to Western governments and commercial bank lenders and to annually rescheduled debt. The one-year financing package (some $2.5 billion credits to be raised in 1990 in the West) suggested by the Polish government in late 1989 and probably debt reduction negotiations with the Polish creditors in the early 1990s will not resolve the Polish creditworthiness problem (to be discussed in more detail in the next section and p. 99). *Hungary* rapidly increased its borrowing and debt levels in the second half of the 1980s, inducing further pressure on its domestic economy and the 'tax on GNP' to be paid abroad. Liquidity difficulties were imminent and a debt consolidation in the form of refinancing was to be expected in 1990–91. *Bulgaria* also considerably increased borrowings and its debt level continued to grow. The Bulgarian financial position was a cause for concern in 1988–90. *The Soviet Union*, the *GDR* and *Czechoslovakia* did not belong among 'debt problem' countries in the late 1980s. However, the borrowing of the Soviet Union rapidly rose in 1987–8 and if this trend continues convertible currency debt will put a heavy burden on the Soviet external balance in the early 1990s. In addition to this the Soviet Union is experiencing serious problems at present related to the repayment of credits it extended to many developing countries. My estimates suggest that these Soviet credits exceed $60 billion. *Romania* continued rigorously to reduce debt in the late 1980s but the economic and debt management of the country is not favourably viewed by the Western financial community.[5]

It has to be stressed, however, that in contrast to the first half of the 1980s the rise of debt in Eastern Europe (except Romania) in 1985–8 was a result not only of borrowing for balance of payments adjustment but also of a valuation effect resulting from the devaluation of the US dollar (which increased the dollar value of non-dollar liabilities in 1986–8). No precise calculations on the valuation effect of non-dollar convertible currency denominated liabilities on debt levels could be made because of lack of published detailed information on the currency composition of Western government and commercial bank loans to Eastern Europe. Some estimates suggest that the non-dollar liabilities accounted for some 50 per cent in 1981–5 (Zloch-Christy, 1988, p. 62). Assuming that this composition of the Eastern European convertible currency debt remained unchanged in 1985–8, one might suggest that some 12 per cent of the growth of net debt in that period was a result of valuation effect.

How realistic is it to expect that Poland and Hungary will restore their creditworthiness in the medium term?

According to the UN Economic Commission for Europe Poland expected to eliminate convertible currency current account deficits by the end of the 1980s or 1990.[6] Poland's governor at the World Bank stated that his country aims to bring its external payments into equilibrium by 1991 (*The Financial Times*, 29 September 1988, p. 6). Poland has improved its relations with the Western commercial banks and governments and has been an active member of both major international financial institutions (the IMF and the World Bank) for almost three years. It reached new rescheduling agreements with commercial banks in 1987–8. The preliminary agreement of July 1987 was on medium and long-term debt due between 1988 and 1993; the repayments were spread over fifteen years (in contrast to all previous agreements which have maturities between $6\frac{1}{2}$ and 11 years). The rescheduling agreement of July 1988 was achieved after more than nine months of negotiations and at very favourable terms for Poland (compared to the previous agreements and to the recent reschedulings of Latin American countries).[7] Debt relief covered $9 billion due in 1988–93, maturity 15 years, interest rate spread of 13/16 of a point over

LIBOR (*The Financial Times*, 20 July 1988, p. 20). Poland reached a new rescheduling agreement with Paris Club, but failed to come to an agreement with the individual Paris Club countries in 1988. No new Paris Club agreement was achieved in 1989 because no agreement was reached with the IMF. The Polish finance minister stated in early 1989 that his government was considering a settlement with the West German government on the so-called 'jumbo credit' of D-Mark 1 billion advanced in the 1970s to Poland and never repaid. This settlement would contribute to the improvement of relations with the other Western governments and the provision of government credits (to Poland) (*The Financial Times*, 25 February 1989, p. 2).

After the election of the non-communist Solidarity-led government in Poland, relations with Western governments, international financial institutions and commercial banks further improved. The European Community called for the provision from the EIB of more than $600 million government credits in 1990. The West German government announced that it was willing to guarantee credits to the amounts of several billion D-Mark related to convertible-currency earning investment projects in Poland; one of the proposals was to convert the D-Mark 1 billion 'jumbo credit' into Polish zlotys for investment (*The Economist*, 30 September 1989, p. 47). Austria suggested several new loans related to convertible-currency earning projects. In late 1989 France offered $23 million government credit and the United Kingdom some $40 million, provided that an agreement between Poland and the IMF was reached. Japan, Canada, the United States, Switzerland and the Scandinavian countries have also suggested new credits for Poland. The World Bank and the IMF in late 1989 considered several loans for industrial, agricultural and transportation projects and for balance of payments adjustment, which were then approved in early 1990. The Bretton Woods institutions made commitments for the first credits to Poland (US$360 million project loans from the World Bank and some US$700 million stabilisation from the IMF). Poland approached Western governments also for a stabilisation fund (grant) for the amount of US$1 billion in order to build up her foreign exchange reserves and support the fixed exchange rate policy in early 1990 (*World Bank News*, 8 February 1990).

Hungary borrowed heavily in 1984–88. Among the Eastern European countries Hungary and the Soviet Union (1987–8) were the most active borrowers on the Eurocurrency market. However, in contrast to the Soviet Union its main debt and creditworthiness indicators have shown rapid deterioration in recent years (as discussed in the previous section). The total borrowing (including IMF stand-by credit) of

Hungary in 1988 amounted to more than $1.3 billion; preliminary data suggest that the total borrowing in 1989 was more than $1.5 billion (the last tranche of the IMF stand-by credit was not disbursed in 1989 because Hungary failed to fulfil some of the stand-by targets negotiated with the IMF). The heavy borrowing in these recent years considerably increased the burden of debt on the economy. The Western financial market shows a certain concern regarding Hungary's creditworthiness. In early 1989 the National Bank of Hungary was seeking a $150 million syndicated credit on terms that suggest increasing concern about the country's liquidity position (*The Financial Times*, 24 February 1989, p. 33). In early 1990 Hungary approached the Western financial community (Bretton Woods institutions, governments and commercial banks) for new creditors. The President of the Hungarian National Bank stated again that his country wants to avoid rescheduling of the external debt: 'We need refinancing of maturities, not rescheduling' (*The New York Times*, 6 March, p. 7). The former Hungarian communist party leader Karoly Grosz in April 1989 made an (unprecedented) statement that the domestic economy was in a 'very critical' situation and 'was close to the point at which the mass debt becomes unmanageable' see *The Financial Times*, 12 April 1989, p. 3).

As was mentioned earlier, in late 1989 the European Community, the USA, Canada, Japan, Austria, Switzerland and others announced loan packages to Hungary to help the process of political and economic liberalization. Many Western countries are increasingly interested in direct investment in Hungary. The so-called 'First Hungarian Fund' was established by a group of Western financiers and the National Bank of Hungary with the prospect of taking direct equity or equity-related investments in Hungarian enterprises with a focus on start-up firms, joint ventures and some of the state-run sector exporting to convertible currency countries (*The Financial Times*, 22 September 1989, p. 26).

Western aid packages for Hungary and Poland are of crucial importance for the support of the market-oriented economic reforms in the two countries. But there is little evidence that the creditworthiness of Hungary and Poland will be dramatically improved in the early 1990s. It is worth mentioning here that the 1982 'bridge loans' helped Hungary to avoid reschedulings of the debt but they did not solve the problem; they only put it off for a time. The improvement in creditworthiness of Hungary and Poland depends crucially on the success of the present economic reforms. And it is obvious that it would take time to see this improvement given the fact that the economy itself evolves through time.

Hungary and Poland were a cause for serious concern in the late 1980s and still are in the early 1990s. Starting from their current base, it seems unlikely that Poland and Hungary will be able to restore a balance of payments equilibrium in the medium term, or to put it differently, Poland's and Hungary's road back to creditworthiness will be long. How long? It is difficult to give a clear-cut answer to this question. Obviously access to Western capital markets will ease the tension in their external balance, but of crucial importance for the two countries is an increase in exports to the West and, in particular, to the European Community and EFTA. New agreements with these trade blocks and probably affiliation with the European Community or membership in EFTA would create a sound basis for increase of exports to the West. However, treaties with the European Community and EFTA would not be enough. Hungary and Poland must generate export capacity and be able to compete on the Western markets. The answer to this problem is very simple: successful introduction and implementation of the radical reform measures. After some two years of political and economic stability foreign investments in these countries will increase, which is also a very important factor for the improvement of their creditworthiness. Privatization, the liberalization of the foreign trade system and the existence of an unified exchange rate and currency convertibility would also give a very strong impetus to exports to the West.

Poland obviously will not continue to pursue an import restrictions policy, which indicates that the trade balance and the current account are likely to remain negative in the transition years. A current account surplus may be achieved in the early 1990s, but it would not have much affect on total debt. Access to IMF, World Bank and the (London based) European Bank for Reconstruction and Development funds for Poland and Hungary could ease the tension in external payments, but the debt levels would remain high and new reschedulings of Poland's debt will be necessary. Reschedulings might become necessary as a form of debt consolidation also for Hungary. The Western financial community is no more optimistic about the debt management of the country than it was in 1982–86.

There are suggestions for the reduction (by about one half) or even for a deeper debt relief on the Polish debt to Paris Club and commercial bank creditors. Harvard Professor Jeffrey Sachs argues that Poland's debt is unserviceable until the end of 1990 and is substantially unpayable in the longer term (*The Financial Times*, 26 September 1989, p. 23; *The Challenge*, January–February 1990, p. 29). If one assumes that such agreements could be achieved between Poland and its creditors it would mean that Poland will service some 20 per cent of its debt in the future (i.e. as much as in the period 1981–9). But this again will not be the only solution to the Polish creditworthiness problem in the medium and long term, because new debt will accumulate very fast. Debt reduction programmes will be difficult to negotiate for Poland because Hungary and Bulgaria (in Eastern Europe) and other heavily indebted developing countries would have similar proposals.

To pay their external debts (even under debt reduction schemes), Poland and Hungary need to restructure their economies and to achieve a rate of growth which would enable them to meet debt obligations without increasing the burden of debt on their future economic performance. But each country still lacks a blueprint for reform in industry. The former Polish prime minister appointed in 1988, M. Rakowski, stated that he would be happy to learn from the British prime minister how to deal with unprofitable industries. He pointed out further that his country's main economic problems were 'inappropriate pay, insufficient raw materials and bad organization' (*The Financial Times*, 29 October 1988, p. 2). There is little evidence that the structural adjustment policies in Hungary and Poland (with strong support from the World Bank) would increase the production and competitiveness of exportables in the medium term. But as F. Havasi, one of the most senior Hungarian politicians, stressed some years ago, structural changes in industry could not by themselves solve the problems (*The Financial Times*, 26 June 1986, p. 2).

The national economies of Poland and Hungary are in a crisis situation. Both countries are facing serious liquidity (and potentially insolvency) problems. The deflationary economic policies and the austerity programmes during the 1980s do not raise hopes that Poland and Hungary will solve their external balance problems in the medium term. The efforts which Poland made to improve its trade and current account balance were too austere to be successful in 1982–9. Hungary's 'overborrowing' in 1985–9 and unsuccessful structural adjustment could easily lead to debt servicing difficulties. Any increase in Poland's capacity to service external debt has been marginal, and the rescheduling process will have to be repeated over and over again. But Poland has introduced, in late 1989, the long-term reforms which give hope that if successfully implemented they will raise its long-term creditworthiness. However, Poland has become and remains a high-cost borrower of capital. This further increases the cost in interest and fees of its external obligations. Hungary's last borrowings showed some hardening of credit conditions. Such are the indicators that debt difficulties will be inherent in the economic development of Poland and Hungary and that it would not be realistic to expect an abatement of Poland's and Hungary's external balance problems in the medium term (unless some debt relief measures were accepted for the two countries).

Credit–debtor policy strategies in East–West financial relations

The debt crisis of the Eastern European countries in the late seventies and early eighties was a consequence of excessive borrowing, of the inefficient use of borrowed funds arising from economic mismanagement in those countries and of weakness in the international lending system. In the early 1980s Soviet officials contended that Poland's 'financial plight should be regarded as a shared responsibility between East and West'[8] and many Western businessmen and scholars stressed in their analysis that the Polish debt resulted from Western as well as Eastern shortcomings.

That proposition invokes the relationship between Western creditors and their Eastern European debtors. Are the Eastern European countries pursuing an import-led or growth-cum-debt policy at present? Is overborrowing similar to that of the 1970s likely in the early 1990s? Is there any evidence to expect a new debt crisis in the medium term?

Such questions require a brief discussion of present *creditor policy*. After 1983, and in particular after 1984, Western financial markets, impressed by the strong and effective efforts at adjustment made by the Eastern European countries (other than Poland), considerably increased their lending to Eastern Europe on terms which became increasingly competitive, but in time came to show a tendency to discriminate among them. As discussed in the preceding sections, Poland's access to the market was precluded until late 1989; Romania refused to take new credits,[9] and there was some hardening of the lending terms to Hungary. Uncertainty about the prospect of Soviet economic reform and the Soviet liquidity difficulties in early 1990 created a cautious attitude among Western businessmen in doing business with the USSR. Some estimates suggest delays of US$1–2 billion in payments for Soviet imports from the West (*The Financial*

Times 25 May 1990, p. 4). Japanese and Italian firms held up their deliveries to the Soviet Union in early 1990. However, as mentioned earlier, lending to the Soviet Union rose rapidly in 1988 and might be estimated between $7 and $9 billion. A West German banker stated that for good projects in the Soviet Union there are 'unlimited' financing recourses (*Der Spiegel*, 17 October 1988, p. 137). But British and particularly United States banks have rather conservative views in their lending policy towards the Soviet Union and Eastern Europe at present. There was criticism in the US Senate of West German and Japanese lending and suggestions for a harder line in lending to Eastern Europe (*The Financial Times* 20 June 1988, p. 3). Influential US congressmen have stated that legislation should be prepared which would penalize the United States subsidiaries of foreign banks which provide credits to the Soviet Union (*The Financial Times*, 2 November 1988, p. 4). After the Italian government granted a $750 million credit to the Soviet Union on very favourable terms (7 per cent to 7.5 per cent interest rates, compared to the 'consensus' rates agreed within the OECD of 8 to 9 per cent for the Soviet Union), there was a debate also in Italy on the scale of concessions for *perestroika* in the Soviet Union (*The Financial Times* 16 November 1988, p. 7).

It would hence be right to expect that further bank-to-bank and publicized loans will continue for Eastern Europe, but wrong to conclude that such operations are indicative of a major revival of Western lending to Eastern Europe similar to that of the 1970s.

The Eastern European borrowers were aware of their, to some extent, favoured position on the market in the second half of the 1980s and are pursuing a policy to take advantage of this position and to obtain better borrowing terms. However, in early 1990 there was a rapid deterioration of the external balance of the region.

There are seven main features in the *Eastern European borrowing policy*.

First, increased borrowing from neutral countries (Austria, Switzerland), Japan and Australia, indicating a desire to avoid any dependence (financial or political) associated with the provision of the borrowed funds.[10] However, the Soviet Union, Poland (in late 1989) and Hungary received major credits from West Germany, Italy, the United Kingdom, the USA and others.

Secondly, borrowing mainly for balance of payments adjustment associated with cuts in Western imports. The reductions of late 1986 to 1988 resulted from the deterioration in the East European terms of trade stemming from the structure of foreign trade (manufactures dominating Eastern European imports, while primary materials, including fuels, weigh heavily in the composition of their exports).

Third, efforts to control the net debt level. But the assets fell and the net liabilities increased. However, Poland and Romania added $0.5 billion and $0.3 billion respectively to their assets in 1987.[11]

Fourth, increased reliance on bank-to-bank credits and reduction of publicized borrowing (except for Hungary and the Soviet Union in 1988 and 1989).

Fifth, a tendency to seek funding more on purely commercial credit markets than through officially guaranteed credits (except for Hungary, Poland and the Soviet Union). No single explanation applies, but it must be noted that the consensus interest rates which apply to guaranteed credits have remained above current commercial rates for several currencies.

Sixth, significant expansion in the forfeit market and the operation of an active and liquid secondary market in forfeit paper. Eastern Europe accounted for 35–40 per cent of that market's activity in 1987–8.[12] However, the deterioration in the external balance in Eastern Europe in early 1990 affected a decline in the forfeit market operations.

Last, diversification of borrowing instruments, particularly for Hungary and the Soviet Union, such as floating rate notes, currency swaps and Eurobonds.

The conclusion is justified that overborrowing similar to that of the 1970s appears unlikely in the light of the chosen constraints of both Eastern European countries and particularly the Western lenders. The debt situation (except for Poland) has been manageable in the late 1980s, there is rapid accumulation of debt but one may optimistically suggest that there is little evidence to expect a new debt crisis in the early 1990s given the access of Eastern European countries to the Western financial markets. However, liquidity difficulties might arise in the region and particularly in Hungary and Bulgaria. The Eastern European countries will want to remain 'cautious borrowers' according to the Hungarian banker J. Fekete,[13] although in his own country's case borrowing policy has not been 'cautious' from 1986 to 1989.

The restrictions on Western imports in 1986–9 indicate that Eastern Europe does not at present pursue an import-led and growth-cum-debt economic policy. It has to be pointed out, however, that a further and drastic reduction of Western imports does not appear likely in the early 1990s, given the plans for modernization and structural change in the economies after the austerity period in 1981–3. This can be proposed with some certainty for the Soviet Union, Poland, Hungary and Bulgaria, but with less assurance for the GDR, Romania and Czechoslovakia. In the case of the Eastern Europe Five (without the GDR) one can indicate two main long-term borrowing strategies: (1) capital imports for structural adjustment and for increasing export capacity to the West; (2) capital imports for producing exportables to the Soviet Union and the realization of cooperation goals within the CMEA area.[14]

Considering the serious difficulties in reforming the CMEA and the policy of the Soviet Union to intensify its economic relations with Western countries, rather than with CMEA, the second strategy does not appear plausible in the early 1990s. A Comecon summit planned for March 1989 in Prague was postponed because of growing differences about economic and trade reforms (common market, convertibility, political reforms and others) particularly among Hungary, Czechoslovakia, East Germany and Romania (*The Financial Times* 28 February 1989, p. 2). The following CMEA summits showed no indication that the economic organization of the Eastern European countries was being redefined to face the challenges of the 1990s.

3   The financing of East–West trade

The balance of payments difficulties of the Eastern European countries in the 1970s which culminated in the debt crisis in 1981 have considerably influenced the forms of financing East–West trade during the 1980s. Disruptions of external financing in the early 1980s were an important cause of the surge in countertrade agreements. The economic reforms and the plans for modernization of the industrial stocks in most of the CMEA countries in the mid and late 1980s gave an impetus to joint ventures and cooperation agreements. New forms of financing became important, for example, international financial institutions' funds, leasing, and funds raised on the international securities markets. This chapter is concerned with the impact of the external debt difficulties of the Eastern European countries and the impact of the economic reforms on the forms of financing East–West trade in the late 1980s and in the 1990s.[1]

Overview

There are a variety of forms of East–West trade financing. Scholars, bankers and businessmen differ in their classification of these forms. It is not a goal of my analysis to go into detail in discussing the differences. The present section is an attempt to systematize and clarify the relevant terminology used. Special attention is given to the trade settlement techniques.

The special trade settlement techniques found increasing acceptance with the Soviet Union and the other Eastern European countries in their trade with the industrialized nations during the 1980s. They were developed because of the recurring shortages of foreign exchange in Eastern Europe. The CMEA countries have increasingly linked the supplier's sales to his purchase of their goods in order (among other things) to minimize outflow of limited convertible currency reserves. The settlement techniques may be classified as:

1 commercial compensation, such as countertrade (barter, counter-purchase, buy-backs) and multilateral trade accords;
2 production compensation, in the context of joint ventures and long-term cooperation agreements;
3 financial compensation, such as clearing/switch and 'transit' deals, export-leasing, export-factoring, and forfeiting.

Some of the forms of financing of East–West Trade discussed in the present study – suppliers' credits, international financial institutions' funds, funds raised on the international securities markets and others – do not fit into the category of the above mentioned settlement techniques and are analysed as separate forms.

Commercial compensation

Countertrade

Countertrade is a term which denotes any one of a wide range of commercial compensation arrangements for international trade and investment projects, the common feature of which is that the financing is denominated partially or entirely in the form of commodities instead of money.[2] According to a GATT analysis of the mid-1980s some 8 per cent of world trade involved countertrade (*The Financial Times*, 7 February 1985, p.1). Many developing countries require 100 per cent countertrade in order to reduce trade imbalances and foster exports. Indonesia, for example, frequently insists on 100 per cent counterpurchase of non-oil domestic goods as a condition of purchasing goods itself (and has some of the most specific countertrade regulations yet seen). According to the United Nations more than ninety countries conduct countertrade today.[3] Western businessmen state that in the late 1980s and 1990s, what really determines whether an exporter closes a deal is not so much the goods he has to sell as the range of finance packages he has to offer. In order to participate in international trade on a major scale many Western firms are prepared to engage in countertrade. Developing countries and most of the Eastern European countries are regions where it is in most cases the only way to sell.

The Eastern European countries advocated and pioneered the use of countertrade arrangements in international business. According to an OECD study the countertrade deals account for some 15 per cent of

East–West trade.[4] However, in interviews, Western European firms (Austrian, German and British) state a figure in a range between 35 per cent and 45 per cent. Since full and reliable statistics on countertrade are not available, this 'field' information seems to me to be realistic.

Among the commercial compensation settlements countertrade is the more generally used form in East–West trade. The main characteristics of a countertrade deal is that the parties' contracts are separate, but linked together, specifying the exports and the payments due in convertible currency, and the imports to be purchased for approximately the same amount in convertible currency; the importer may be a third party and banks may be involved as short-term lenders when the two transactions are not exactly synchronized. The main motives for countertrade of the Eastern European countries, as in the case of the developing countries, are (and will be in the future): firstly, to acquire imports in the absence of foreign exchange or credit; secondly, to develop new exports or new export markets by passing all or part of the marketing role (distribution channels and experience) to the Western supplier (market penetration); thirdly, to acquire technology and know-how; fourthly, to balance trade bilaterally, and lastly, to overcome protectionist barriers in the Western countries.

Protectionist measures are growing in the Western industrialized countries (see p. 93), and this increases the difficulties (among others) which Eastern European countries have in trying to sell their products during the 1990s. The pressure for further protectionism is encouraging countertrade between East and West. Countertrade is a consequence of the erosion of the commitment to an open trading system in the world and particularly in the Western countries. With more barriers and less trade commercial compensation settlements are likely to be more frequent in the future.[5]

Three forms of countertrade in the East–West relations will be discussed here: barter, counterpurchase and buy-backs. It has to be noted, however, that there exist many variants on these three types, and many institutional complications.[6] The main principles underlying the differences between the individual East–West countertrade deals in the present study are firstly, the time factor in the exchange of the two groups of goods, and secondly, the types of goods exchanges, and their economic or technical relation to one another.

Barter Countertrade in East–West trade is often referred to as barter, 'modern barter' or 'barter-like trade', which at some point is

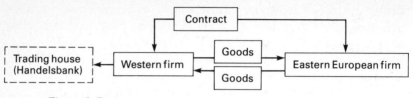

Figure 2 Barter

misleading with regard to the large majority of countertrade settlements. Actually only a small fraction of these settlements can be viewed as barter. In a barter deal the two groups of goods are exchanged at the same or nearly the same time. In current East–West trade the two sides of a barter are usually executed within one year. Figure 2 illustrates a barter arrangement.

In most cases barter deals include an exchange of Eastern European primary commodities in return for Western manufactured items. After the debt crisis in the early 1980s the East–West barter trade was regarded by both sides to be superior to a 'no trade' situation. However, pure barter transactions are in fact rare at present as opposed to other forms of commercial and production compensation. This trend will continue in the medium and long-term. Barter deals are reported between the GDR, Czechoslovakia, Bulgaria, Romania and Poland, on the one side, and West Germany on the other, and between the Soviet Union and several Western countries (Finland, USA, Norway). Romania is the only Eastern European country at present which insists on relatively more barter with the West. Romania concluded in early 1989, a barter arrangement amounting to $200 million with West Germany for delivery of domestic motors, ships, tankers, furniture and glassware in return for three long-range 767 aircraft from Boeing (*The Financial Times*, 6 February 1989, p. 4). In early 1989, the Soviet Union signed a $2.6 billion barter agreement with three Western partners (United States, Norway, Bermuda) involving eighty-five ships (*The Financial Times*, 14 April 1989, p. 6).

The barter deals will remain important in the relationship between the Eastern European countries and the developing countries in the next decade; for example, oil supplies from the Middle East in return for machinery and equipment, including arms, etc. Their significance in East–West trade will be marginal.

Counterpurchase In a counterpurchase arrangement one party (Eastern European firm) imports a commodity and the selling or

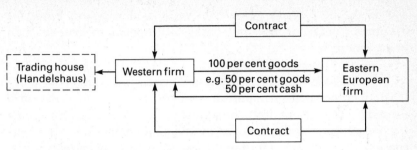

Figure 3 Counterpurchase

exporting party (Western firm) undertakes an obligation to purchase from the first party commodities with a value equal to a contracted portion of the original sale value at a future point in time. The temporal separation of the two sides of the arrangement is the distinguishing factor between barter and counterpurchase. Counterpurchase is usually executed within three to five years after the original sale. Figure 3 illustrates a general counterpurchase settlement.

The level of compensation in East–West counterpurchase agreements is usually no higher than 90 per cent. The highest compensation levels are typically found in deals with Poland (60–90 per cent) and Romania (60–80 per cent). Counterpurchase agreements with compensation levels of 100 per cent (known as parallel countertrade) are relatively underpresented in East–West trade. The goods which may be purchased (by a Western firm) in order to fulfil the counterpurchase obligations are typically specified in a shopping list; the goods in this list (manufactured goods, raw materials, consumer goods, etc.) do not usually relate to the goods originally purchased in accordance with the first contract in any technical or immediate economic sense. A third party (trading house) may be also involved in the transaction (e.g. the Western firm assigns the delivery to a trading house).

Counterpurchase agreements between East and West received an impetus in the second half of the 1980s. One of the interesting counterpurchase agreements was signed between the US firm Pepsico and the Soviet Union: Pepsico financed the building of twenty-eight Soviet Pepsi plants in return (partly) for Soviet ships (*The Financial Times*, 29 September 1989, p. 18). Particularly active on the side of the Western countries are West European countries – West Germany, France, Italy, Austria, Finland, the United Kingdom – and Japan, and on the side of Eastern Europe – the Soviet Union, Hungary, the GDR, Poland and Bulgaria. One might expect that this trend will continue also in the next decade. However, most of the Eastern European countries will favour more buy-backs and production compensation (joint ventures).

Buy-backs   In a buy-back commercial compensation one party (Eastern European firm) imports machinery or a complete plant from a second party (Western firm); the second party agrees to buy back some fraction of the output produced by the equipment, and this repurchase finances payment for the original sale. The buy-backs typically require more than five years before the purchases of the second party begin. There is a clear technical relation (in contrast to barter and counterpurchase) between the goods originally purchased and those bought back; however, in some buy-backs economically associated goods may be bought back although they do not originate from the plant and equipment originally sold. As in the case of counterpurchase settlements, two separate contracts are signed. Third parties may participate in the sale of the buy-back goods. Buy-backs in East–West trade are used most often to finance projects in the extractive industries, (oil, gas etc.) the processing and delivering of primary commodities, and to finance heavy manufacture, infrastructure, or tourism (hotel construction projects). The motives of the Eastern European countries for buy-back deals go beyond the shortage of convertible currency or difficulty in obtaining access to capital and commodity markets. Their goals include the modernization of industrial production, the acquisition of new equipment and know-how. Technology transfer is often present in the buy-back arrangements. Buy-backs are sometimes part of medium and long-term industrial policies or sectoral development programmes in Eastern Europe and include elements of investment. Because of their long-term horizons (five, ten years), countertrade commitments become predetermined for several years to come.

Both in East and West a new infrastructure to promote countertrade and particularly counterpurchase and buy-backs has been built up during the 1980s, including specialized intermediaries, trading firms, as well as special countertrade units within international corporations, banks and law firms. Among the Western countries particularly active in this field have been Austria and Germany. Austria has pioneered the buy-backs deals in East–West trade and was the first Western country to sign a buy-back agreement with the Soviet Union (gas-pipeline deal) in 1969; the long-term agreement was renewed in the mid-1980s. A great deal of buy-backs are signed between Austria on the one side and Hungary (hotel construction), the GDR and Poland on the other side. The United Kingdom also has been expanding its countertrade activities in the late 1980s along the lines of promoting trade and economic cooperation with Eastern Europe (particularly with the Soviet Union, Hungary and Poland). Japan, France and Italy promote counterpurchase agreements with Eastern Europe as well. The Japanese firm Toyota announced in early 1990 its decision for a buy-back arrangement, which when implemented will be the largest Japanese investment in the region (*The Financial Times*, 25 May 1990, p. 4). Buy-backs appear to be an important form of financing East–West trade in the 1990s given the policies of the Eastern European countries (as discussed in chapter 1 and the above analysis).

Multilateral trade accords

The multilateral trade accords are known in East–West trade also as 'framework agreements'. These accords between governmental or other representative agencies seek to balance trade flows for a given period and for specified goods. A central settlement account is usually employed, but in contrast to clearing agreements, remaining balances can be settled in convertible currency. The trade accords specify in very general terms the relations between Eastern European and Western partners for a period of several years; special renewable agreements determine the nature, value and timing of the exchanged commodities. At present most of the Eastern European countries have signed such agreements with Western partners (Western Europe, USA, Canada, Japan, Australia). Their significance, however, for (considerably) promoting East–West trade and financial relations in the next decade will be marginal.

Production compensation

Joint ventures

Most of the Eastern European countries (except Romania and the GDR) were encouraging production compensation with the West in the second half of the 1980s. Joint ventures were the most promoted form,[7] in order firstly, to attract investment capital, secondly, to acquire technological know-how, thirdly, to improve marketing (both in the domestic market and foreign markets), and fourthly, to establish an import substitution production. The Soviet academician Aganbe-

gyan (1989, p. 189) stresses that joint ventures 'are of great importance' for broadening the foreign economic relations and international
collaboration of the Soviet Union. The number of East–West ventures
increased from 75 in 1986 to 166 at the end of 1987, Hungary and the
Soviet Union attracting the main interest of Western firms. Total
foreign investments in Eastern Europe reached some $500 million in
1987[8] and the number of joint venture agreements at the end of 1987
was 111 in Hungary, 32 in the Soviet Union, 15 in Bulgaria, 5 in
Romania and 3 in Czechoslovakia (*The Financial Times*, 14 April 1988,
p. 3). The joint venture settlements of Hungary rapidly rose in 1988.
An analysis shows that with West Germany 200 contracts were signed
(*The Economist*, 14 April 1989, p. 57). Some 80 new contracts were
signed with West German firms in 1989 (*The Financial Times*, 12
October 1989, p. 2). The number of joint ventures with Western
countries reached some 600 in 1989, although many of them are small
firms. The main factors stimulating the rapid expansion of the joint
venture agreements in Hungary have been the economic and political
liberalization allowing 100 per cent foreign ownership of Hungarian
firms and also (among others) cheap labour. Sales from joint ventures
per employee are several times higher than the average for Hungarian
industry. (*The Economist*, 21 October 1989, p. 78). The number of
Soviet agreements continued to rise in 1988 and 1989 as well. In a
presentation for Ambrosetti to British businessmen, Academician
Aganbegyan stated that some 115 joint ventures had been signed by
November 1988 and that some 40 new projects were under consideration. West Germany alone proposed some 500 joint ventures in the
Soviet Union in 1988 and it is expected that more than 100 new
agreements will be signed (*Der Spiegel*, 17 October 1988, p. 136). More
than forty British firms negotiated joint ventures with Moscow in 1988
(*The Journal of the British–Soviet Chamber of Commerce*, London, no. 8,
1988: 6). Interviews with Soviet scholars suggest that the signed
agreements on joint ventures with Western partners had reached 329
by the end of 1989. However, it must be stressed that few joint
ventures had actually come into operation. (*The Financial Times*, 20
October 1988, p. 9; *Der Spiegel*, 21 May 1990, p. 125). The main
partners of the Soviet Union are firms from West Germany and the
United States. Finland is increasing her interest in establishing many
joint ventures in the Soviet Union. The joint ventures are in petrochemical production, medical technology, computers, motor cars,
training and consultancy, banking (with Germany), light industry,
publishing, as well as others. The Soviet Union in line with its policy to

intensify economic relations with East Asian countries proposed a 'zone of joint enterprise' in the Asia-Pacific region and suggested to Japan and China the initiation of major economic programmes (*The Financial Times*, 12 October 1988, p. 4). The Soviet Union is also considering the creation of free zones – Far East (Vladivostok), Armenia, The Baltic states, Leningrad, Novgorod – for foreign investment (industrial, commercial, finance) and is studying the experience of China in this field. There is discussion on the introduction of parallel currency in these zones which will be convertible for non-residents and consequently for residents. A decision on such zones is expected in 1990. The Soviet authorities announced in late 1988 a wide review of regulations and legislation affecting joint ventures (the last legislation dated from January 1987). Preceded by hints that Western foreign partners should be allowed to control up to 80 per cent of shares in joint ventures, against the 49 per cent of the 1987 law (*The Financial Times*, 4 November 1988, p. 2), the regulations which emerged imposed no specific limit on the Western equity holding; a foreign citizen can be chairman of the joint venture. In Poland the new Foreign Investment Law of 1 January 1989 allows foreign partners to hold 100 per cent of shares in joint ventures (as in Hungary); the contribution of foreign partners cannot be lower than 20 per cent of equity (Article 2). Another change in the Polish Law is that the joint company shall sell 15 per cent (previously 25 per cent) of its foreign currency export proceeds to the Polish Foreign Exchange Bank; 'in economically justified cases' the rate of sale may be lower (Article 19). In Bulgaria regulations also allow for a majority share held by a foreign partner. Czechoslovakia, the GDR and Romania accept only a minority foreign share. In Poland, Hungary and (as mentioned) in the Soviet Union the chairman of the joint venture can be a foreign citizen. The individual countries' law provides for different taxation regulations and legal forms of the joint enterprises. The Hungarian law is the most liberal among the CMEA countries.

The interest of Western businessmen in establishing joint ventures in Eastern Europe, and particularly in the Soviet Union, has been increasing in 1987–9. Many international conferences on promoting joint ventures in Eastern Europe were held both in East and West. The Soviet Union and Hungary have signed the first consultancy agreement with Western firms to provide advice on and assist foreign companies in establishing joint ventures in the CMEA countries. One of these agreements is the consultancy contract between the Soviet firm Vneshconsult and the British consultancy firm Ernst & Whinney, signed in January 1989. Ernst & Whinney has a representing office in Hungary as well. Another agreement is on the establishing of a joint venture between the Austrian firm AWT, the Rockefeller Company, the Hungarian Credit Bank and the Hungarian Foreign Trade Bank, for promoting joint venture projects between interested Western partners and Hungarian firms, signed in April 1989. (*The Financial Times*, 20 April 1989, p. 7)

A British businessman stated in a conference in London in 1988 that he was enthusiastic about establishing joint ventures in Eastern Europe, and particularly in the Soviet Union, because these

> ventures really are an opportunity at present. They are not an opportunity in the classic sense of being automatically attractive investment in a politically stable environment ... The joint venture approach enables a company to emphasise its unique features in its relations with its partners ... The joint venture approach also opens the door to many companies without existing trade relations with the USSR who ... prefer to investigate a long-term investment opportunity rather than a short-term export opportunity.[9]

According to the chief executive of the East section of the Chamber of the West German industries (Ostausschuss der Deutschen Wirtschaft), in the 1990s an extraordinary boom in joint venture business with the Soviet Union and Eastern Europe might occur (*Der Spiegel*, 17 October 1989, p. 137).

The main motives of the Western partners in establishing joint ventures in Eastern Europe are:

potential cost savings (relatively cheaper labour cost);

after-sale advantage;

advantage of a pioneer;

internal exports and new market shares.[10]

In the USA, Japan and Italy the most active in establishing joint venture business with Eastern Europe are the big firms and corporations while in Germany and Austria it is typically the middle and small-scale enterprises. The small and middle firms take more risks than the giant enterprises which are 'hesitant' in West Germany and Austria. One might speculate that the big firms would like to avoid big projects with the Soviet Union because of considerations for future competition from Soviet production (*Der Spiegel*, 17 October 1988, p. 137). In a hearing to the Joint Economic Committee of the US Congress it was stated that Western potential co-producers in joint ventures with the Soviet Union are 'not particularly interested in creating another competitor'; the Western firms have different objectives from the Soviet firms – the West wants to open up the huge Soviet market and the Soviet Union is looking to develop a capability to ultimately compete with the West.[11]

Although the number of signed joint venture contracts rose rapidly in 1987–9,[12] as was mentioned earlier, not many of them came into operation. It has to be noted here that the Soviet Union has been promoting production compensation with the West in the recent two to three years. But Tzarist Russia had relatively little experience with free enterprise before 1917 and after more than seventy years of Soviet communism, private initiative and risk-taking in the Soviet Union were thoroughly suppressed. Although many Western businessmen are enthusiastic about joint venture projects with the Soviet Union and Eastern Europe, particularly Poland and Hungary, actually a relatively small fraction of Western firms are engaged or considering such deals with this region at present. A study by a British marketing research firm stated that its survey of 688 companies in Europe and the USA showed that three-quarters of them traded with Eastern Europe, but only 11 per cent of those were involved in joint ventures; only 15 per cent of the companies were considering new arrangements for industrial cooperation, including joint ventures (*The Financial Times*, 3 February, 1989, p. 4). Most Western businessmen still do not see real changes in doing business with the CMEA countries. There exist barriers in establishing joint ventures in Eastern Europe quickly and efficiently and with a quick return.

The general attitude of Western businessmen not only towards the Soviet Union, but also the other Eastern European countries is that there are many uncertainties in the economic reforms in Eastern Europe and the legislation of these countries is inflexible. They perceive problems in the following areas of joint venture agreements:

proportion of capital provided by each partner;

managerial controls;

raw materials and equipment supplies to the joint East–West venture within the (modified) centralized Eastern European planned economy;

setting of the selling price;

guarantees for the repatriation of profits for the Western partners;

lack of commodity and currency convertibility;

excessive bureaucratic procedures and slow decision-making in Eastern Europe;

uncertainties in providing guarantees for the joint projects;

lack of infrastructure in Eastern Europe.

Most Western companies point out that the lack of commodity and currency convertibility, and the complications connected with the provision of guarantees for the projects are some of the most serious obstacles in promoting joint ventures in Eastern Europe. Even in imaginative deals for 'import substitution' Western firms (British, German etc.) could not avoid many problems connected with the currency non-convertibility on the trade and current account. 'Import substitution' is so called because the Western partner agrees in advance to receive a part of the savings of convertible currency for the Soviet Union which results from obtaining Western products for the joint venture which otherwise had to be imported by the Soviet Union. There is no doubt that attempts to achieve currency and commodity convertibility in Eastern Europe and thereby get credit by having other countries and traders wanting to hold Eastern European currencies would have an enormous impact on increasing East–West trade and joint venture projects. But it is difficult to make any predictions about orders of magnitude since no controlled experiments could be made, along with the fact that the economy (in Eastern Europe) itself evolved through time. It has to be stressed, however, that convertibility *per se* will not gain the Eastern European countries a significant amount of credit without radical market-oriented restructuring of their economies. Foreigners would be interested in holding Eastern European currencies if the trade and joint venture offers were credible and the exchange rates plausibly reflected the CMEA currencies' purchasing power. An American study argues that in the case of the Soviet rouble, foreigners might want to provide credit in hard currency to the Soviet Union at very favourable rates by buying rouble-denominated bonds guaranteed in gold (IMF, *Morning Press*, 11 October 1989).

In the Soviet Union and the other Eastern European countries whether to supply guarantees for joint ventures has not been ruled out and, also, what institutions might offer them. For example, the Soviet Bank for Foreign Economic Affairs could back the joint projects to a certain point, but the branch ministries, and the individual state and cooperative enterprises, which from 1 April 1989 have had the right to make direct contracts with foreign partners, do not have financial backing in convertible currency funds. One of the important questions which remain unanswered in the Soviet and other Eastern European countries' legislation is: what will happen in the case of liquidation of the joint venture?

It might be expected that Eastern European banks will take portfolios in the new joint ventures and will also provide guarantees (in convertible currency) up to a certain point. But the latter prospect is not very bright given the debt problems of most of the Eastern European countries.

Cooperation agreements

The cooperation agreements[13] are long-term settlements between Eastern European and Western firms in a wide area of activities: for the reciprocal delivery of technically related goods such as the supply of an industrial plant paid by the export of part of its output to the supplying (Western) country; co-marketing activities; cooperation (production and marketing) on third markets and others. Western and East European scholars and businessmen differ in their definition of cooperation agreements. It is not a goal of the present analysis to discuss these differences. However, it must be noted here that cooperation agreements are a *broad* type of production compensation settlement which have some elements of countertrade deals (e.g. buy-backs) or joint ventures. The main difference between cooperation agreements and buy-backs is that the long-term cooperation settlement might include many areas (production, marketing, etc.) and be based on more than two individual contracts; in contrast to joint ventures the cooperation agreements do not provide shared control of the enterprise.

Industrial cooperation between East and West began in the 1970s, during the first period of detente. Austria[14] and Germany were actively involved in such agreements with Hungary, the Soviet Union, Romania and Poland. The other Western and East European countries were rather cautious in promoting this form of agreement. Most agreements were in machine building and the chemical industry. However, industrial cooperation in the 1970s did not exceed the frame of licence contracts.[15] In the second half of the 1980s there is a new interest on both sides to promote this form. German, Austrian, British, Japanese and American firms are discussing numerous projects with the Soviet Union, Hungary, Poland and Bulgaria. The development of industrial cooperation is envisaged, for example, in the Programme for Economic and Industrial Cooperation between the Soviet Union and the United Kingdom. One of the cooperation projects is for example, the contract between the Soviet firm Minpribor and the British firm Quest Automation on joint development of automated systems on the basis of Soviet computer technology and British peripheral devices; another contract is between the Soviet firms

Minstankoprom and Minkhimmash, and the British firm G. F. C. Robot Systems on cooperation in the production of painting robots.[16] All of this indicates that industrial cooperation will develop further in the 1990s. However, as in the case of joint ventures, this development will depend on the progress of the economic reforms in Eastern Europe and on the general political and economic climate between East and West.

Financial compensation

Clearing/switch and 'transit' deals

The clearing/switch and 'transit' deals between East and West developed in the 1960s and reached their peak in the early 1970s.[17] Western European countries, and in particular, Austria, Switzerland, Germany and Holland, were the main partners of Eastern Europe. Specialised trading firms, as well as special units within international corporations and banks were established in order to promote these deals. However, the importance of clearing/switch and 'transit' transactions has decreased since the mid-1970s because of the expiration of the bilateral clearing agreements in Europe, and because of the development of other forms of financing East–West trade and access of the CMEA countries to the international capital markets.

The switch transactions typically are based on an unbalanced bilateral clearing account between two countries with 'soft' currencies (an exhausted swing line) and a third party (switcher) in a country with convertible currency. There exist import, export, and finance-switch deals; export- and import-switch deals can be combined and are known in the praxis as 'switch-circuit' (*Doppel*-switch). The switch transactions are relatively complicated techniques and are expensive for Eastern European countries because of the large discount fees paid to the switcher. Debt problems and the shortage of convertible currency in Eastern Europe were the main reasons for these transactions in East–West trade and financing during the 1980s. In the early 1980s, after the 1981 crisis, the switch deals had a relative expansion; with the renewal of Eastern Europe's access to Western capital markets in 1985–6 the importance of these deals decreased again. However, in the late 1980s and in the next decade they will remain as one of the forms of financing East–West trade because of the continuing debt servicing difficulties of most of the CMEA countries and because of the existence of clearing agreements between the individual

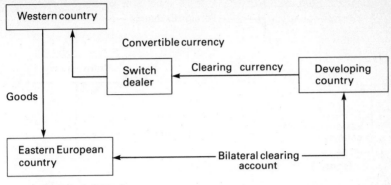

Figure 4 Switch

CMEA countries and numerous developing countries (most of which also face serious debt problems). Figure 4 illustrates a general switch transaction.

A Western country exports to an Eastern European country where no convertible currency is available; the Eastern European country has a clearing agreement with a developing country, which is out of balance in favour of the former. A portion of the clearing balance is bought by a switch dealer (in a Western country) who pays the exporting firm in convertible currency (less discount); the switch dealer sells the clearing 'currency' to another country trading with the particular developing country, or uses it to acquire goods from the latter.

The switch transactions are very often associated in the praxis of East–West trade with the 'transit' deals'; the latter could be actually a reason for the switch. They involve the movement of goods between three countries. The 'transit' deals are known also as 'triangular compensation'. These deals increased in the early 1980s. In interviews, Austrian, German and British firms stated that they will remain an important form of financing for East–West trade in the 1990s for the same reasons as noted in the case of the switch deals. Figure 5 illustrates a general triangular compensation.

In the triangular compensation all transactions are settled in convertible currency. If it is the case that the Eastern European country has a clearing agreement with the third country (typically developing country) the triangular compensation leads to a switch deal. Timing differences in these financial compensation schemes may be bridged by an intermediary who earns a discount from the party receiving early settlement.

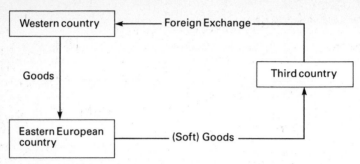

Figure 5 Triangular compensation

Among the West European countries, Austria has been very much involved in 'transit' deals between East and West. It has been an important intermediary for West German exports to Hungary, the Soviet Union, Czechoslovakia and the GDR. The 'transit' deals might be applied more in trade and credit relations between Western European countries (Austria, Switzerland, Germany) and the CMEA region, than between the USA, Japan, Australia and the CMEA in the future. The main reasons for this trend are, firstly, the greater experience which most of the Western European countries have as compared to the rest of the OECD members, and secondly, the favourable climate for increasing trade relations between Eastern Europe (and particularly the Soviet Union) and Western Europe in the medium term.

Export leasing

Another area of financial compensation deals in East–West trade are the leasing agreements. The concept of these transactions is 'paying for use, not ownership'. The Western leasing company (the lessor) is an owner of equipment provided to the Eastern European user (the lessee) which pays rental for its possession and use. In other words, lease purchase transactions in East–West trade relate to the hiring and eventual ownership of assets for use in Eastern Europe. Although it has been an important source of medium-term finance for Western industry and commerce for more than three decades, its application in East–West deals began in the mid-1970s.

Hungary initiated the establishment of the first East–West leasing firms. There are no available statistics on leasing transactions. Interview material indicates that from the beginning of the 1980s, and particularly after 1985, only Hungary, the Soviet Union, Czecho-slovakia, the GDR and Bulgaria have been involved in leasing agreements with Western firms on a relatively small scale. The GDR has increased its deals with West Germany in 1986–8. One might expect that Poland will also be interested in leasing for medium-term finance in the future, given its debt problems and the prospects for improvement in its relations with the Western capital markets. Plans for the modernization of industry in Eastern Europe will require acquisition of capital equipment in the early 1990s. Leasing appears to be one of the best alternatives to outright purchase of equipment in the CMEA countries. There are data which show that Hungary expects, by the early 1990s, that Western machinery and equipment worth $600 million will be leased on the basis of import permits related to the level of expected hard-currency receipts; permits will be granted through competitive lending.[18]

There are three forms of leasing applied in East–West transactions: finance, operating, and residual leasing. A *finance lease* is a lease agreement usually designed to fully amortise the cost of an asset over its useful economic life. The Eastern European firm is not, and will not become, the owner of the leased equipment. Finance leasing deals are referred to as 'full pay out' leases. An *operating lease* is generally the reverse of a finance lease. It is a lease agreement with a residual value; it provides for asset sale to the Eastern European firm at the end of the basic lease period. The *residual value lease* is an agreement where the basic lease period is less than the useful economic life of the asset provided to the Eastern European firm and usually the asset has a realisable market value at the end of this period.

The main benefits for the Eastern European countries in using leasing as a form of financing East–West trade are: (1) 100 per cent financing and flexible rental patterns; (2) stability provided by the fact that these agreements are relatively unaffected by exchange control regulations, exchange rates changes, and credit squeezes with other financing forms; (3) flexibility in financing East–West production compensation agreements; equipment acquired can be self-financing – rentals being generated from the asset's income.

All that indicates that expansion of leasing agreements might be expected in the next decade.

Export-factoring

Export-factoring is a relatively rare form of financing East–West trade at present. There are no available statistics on export-factoring. Hungary was the first East European country which initiated it more than ten years ago. In 1976 a contract was signed between a West German Factor Bank and the Hungarian National Bank; the Hungarian National Bank acts as an import-factor bank and was obliged to take risks of non-payment by the domestic foreign trade enterprises to the Western factor bank. Poland and Bulgaria signed similar contracts in the early 1980s with West German export-factor banks.

Export-factoring is an alternative way of financing East–West trade and provides advantages to Western firms as regards short-term claims (in the range between thirty and ninety days). Export-factoring enables a Western exporter to sell on open credit terms with the benefit of 100 per cent credit cover against non payment. Most Western export-factoring banks which buy Western firms' future short-term claims from deals in a particular CMEA country provide a cash facility of up to 80 per cent of credit covered invoices.

The expected increase of trade relations between East and West in the short and medium-term will provide the grounds for the development of export-factoring as an alternative to short-term financing of East–West business transactions. However, as compared with the other financing forms, its relevance will remain marginal.

Forfeiting

Most of the Eastern European countries preferred to use a forfeit segment of the Western private capital markets along with the unpublicised bank-to-bank credits in the late 1980s (as noted in chapter 2). Forfeiting as a form of financing East–West trade developed rapidly during the 1970s. Austria, Switzerland and Germany have been very active in forfeiting deals with Eastern European countries. The financial institutions operating on the market are banks, the specialised forfeiting units of banks and independent forfeiting firms. The presence of the CMEA countries on the market depends on their creditworthiness. After the 1981 debt crisis, the forfeit markets remained almost precluded for most of the Eastern European countries (except the Soviet Union and Czechoslovakia) in 1982–4.

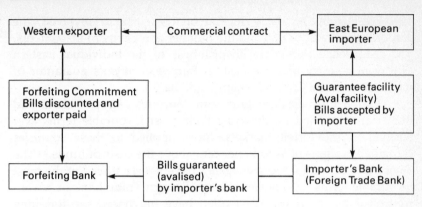

Figure 6 Forfeiting deal

'Forfeiting' or 'a forfeit' is derived from French (*forfait*) meaning 'to surrender something'; in financial transactions meaning to give up rights to payment under a bill. It is a form of financing (East–West) trade where the forfeiting bank purchases an exporter's receivables (bills of exchange or promissory notes), discounting them, usually at a fixed rate without recourse to the exporter; the forfeiting bank either retains the receivables which have the guarantee of payment (typically in the form of separate guarantee or aval) by another internationally known bank (usually an Eastern European foreign trade bank), for presentation at the maturity dates, or sells them in the forfeit market. Forfeiting often involves the syndication of large credits to Eastern Europe. Figure 6 illustrates a general forfeiting transaction.

Forfeiting as a highly flexible form of financing East–West trade is an extra option for Western exporters. However, it should not be seen as being in competition with other export finance schemes, e.g. supplier's or buyer's credits that are used to finance much longer-term multi-million turnkey projects, such as chemical plants, machine building plants, and others. The main benefits for the Eastern European countries in using forfeiting in East–West trade and credit relations are: the possibility of obtaining up to 100 per cent fixed rate finance; flexible repayment schemes; the possibility of obtaining credit in several convertible currencies; the commission paid by the Eastern European importer for the bank guarantee or aval, which typically is less than the commission on a letter of credit; and the finance costs, which based on commercial market interest rates, may be lower than were the deal arranged under OECD consensus arrangements.

The above discussion indicates that the costs of raising funds in

East–West forfeiting deals depend on the currency involved, the amount, the credit period and the number of repayment instalments. The risks relate to the creditworthiness of the individual Eastern European country and the Eastern European buyer's guarantor (if different from the CMEA Foreign Trade Bank).

In 1987–8 most Eastern European countries (except Poland and Bulgaria) succeeded in obtaining their most favourable terms ever reached in the forfeit markets. Rates applied to these countries contained margins of ⅛ to ¼ per cent above the costs of funds.[19] The Soviet Union's and Czechoslovakia's papers were traded at the most favourable terms. The Soviet Union's Foreign Trade Bank or Soviet-controlled banks in the West often have purchased the forfeiting claims themselves taking advantage of the relatively low fixed rates. According to OECD estimates the East European share of Western forfeit deals increased from some 10 per cent in 1984 to 25 per cent in 1986 and 35–40 per cent in 1987–8.[20] A further expansion of activities in the primary and secondary forfeiting markets for Eastern European papers might be expected in the short and medium term. It has to be stressed, however, that the position of the individual countries in the market will vary depending on their creditworthiness.

Other financing

The forms of East–West financing are susceptible to diversification in line with the general developments in international finance. Eastern European members of the IMF and the World Bank, as well as new members will have access to the funds of these institutions. Some of the CMEA countries have borrowed on the international securities markets in 1984–9. Suppliers' credits, project financing, lines of credit and free credits have been important forms of financing in the 1970s and in the 1980s. Since the author has analysed developments in these forms in previous publications, this section provides a brief discussion on these issues.[21]

Supplier's credits, project financing and lines of credit

Supplier's credits have been an important and traditional form of financing East–West trade. They gained in importance in the early 1980s as a consequence of the debt crisis in the region. In 1982–84 supplier's credits were the predominent alternative in East–West trade and finance. Supplier's credits are known also as commercial credits

(Handelskredite). These can be: short-term (30 days), medium-term (1–3 years) and long-term (more than 3 years). The medium and long-term commercial credits are provided to finance investment goods deliveries to Eastern Europe. The debt servicing problems of Poland and Romania in the early 1980s caused a cautious attitude among Western banks in providing supplier's credits to these countries in favour of project financing. There are no available statistics on commercial credits in East–West trade. Estimates for Austria show that, for example, their share in the total volume of Austrian credits to Eastern Europe amounted to 36 per cent in 1980 and 17 per cent in the mid-1980s.[22] According to market sources the supplier's credits will expand in the short and medium-term and will remain one of the main forms of financing East–West trade in the next decade.

Project financing and lines of credit are favoured by Western creditors because they allow for controls on the use of borrowed funds. *Project financing* relates to investment projects in Eastern Europe; the repayment scheme of the credits is between ten and fifteen years. The Western credits provided are often guaranteed by the export credit agencies of the OECD countries. Export credits have been an important factor of OECD economic policy since the mid-1970s and particularly since the beginning of the 1980s; they are one of the government supported measures for promoting export industries in the Western countries. However, the Eastern European countries insisted in the late 1980s on export credits with fixed interest rates below market rates. As was noted (in chapter 2 and p. 68) they prefer bank-to-bank credits and forfeiting. In other words, it is not a question of a shortage of export credits, but of East European demand being relatively weak.

The economic reforms in Eastern Europe create a favourable climate for the expansion of project financing. In a conference in London in early 1989 a representative of the Soviet controlled Moscow Narodny Bank stated that numerous projects were under consideration. However, lending for the projects at present is on the basis of a precise input–output analysis and on the cashflow of the particular project; project financing is not any more a 'supplier, contractive' business. Very often project financing is accompanied by a countertrade (typically counterpurchase) agreement. The Soviet Bank for Foreign Economic Relations (previously Foreign Trade Bank) is very selective in providing guarantees at present, and their number has decreased. It is possible to obtain guarantees from the Soviet branch ministries but they represent only a part of the necessary cover. For Poland Western banks provided credits for project financing in the late 1980s only if a 100 per cent Polish government guarantee was available. As in the case of the joint ventures, one of the main problems in developing project financing between East and West is the Eastern European currency and commodity non-convertibility.

Lines of credit usually provide credit from the lending bank to the borrowing bank of the Eastern European country under which the lender disburses direct to the exporter against agreed documentation. The credits are provided only for exports from the exporting country. The lines of credit can be with or without export credit guarantee cover. The biggest banks in the West, and particularly in Western Europe have lines of credit with the individual Eastern European countries. However, British, French and Italian banks are more restrictive in opening such lines with CMEA countries, than German, Austrian and Swiss banks. For example, one of the biggest British commercial banks, Barclays Bank, had lines of credit only with the Soviet Union, Czechoslovakia, the GDR and Bulgaria in the late 1980s; the 'high risk' countries Hungary, Poland and Romania were excluded from this financing scheme. The lines of credit are available for contracts over £10 million ($17 million).

Free financing

The free credits to Eastern Europe flourished during the 1970s. The 1981 debt crisis precluded the access of most of the Eastern European countries to the market. But, after 1984 the provision of free credits to the CMEA region increased again (see chapter 2). Free credits are mainly funds raised in the national Western capital markets (swaps agreements, unpublicised bank-to-bank credits) or borrowings on the Euromarket. The Soviet Union and the other Eastern European countries have established their institutions for activities in the Western capital markets in the recent twenty-five years. The CMEA international banks (International Bank for Economic Cooperation and the International Investment Bank) undertake borrowings of free credits. CMEA controlled Western banks: Moscow Narodny Bank (London), Banque Commercialle pour l'Europe du Nord (Paris), Wozchodbank (Zurich), Handelsbank (Frankfurt/Main), and others, very often participate in Euromarket syndications. According to market sources it was expected, in the late 1980s that most of the Eastern European countries (except for Poland, Hungary and Bulgaria) would continue to be active on the Western national capital markets and the Euromarket in the short and medium term. The unpublicised bank-to-bank credits would be preferred to the Euromarket credits because of their comparative low costs of borrowing at present. In 1987–8 some of the CMEA countries (the Soviet Union, Czechoslovakia) obtained bank-to-bank credits on very favourable terms – for example eight years with six years grace at interest rate ⅛ over LIBOR. The access of Eastern Europe to the Western free credits will depend principally on their creditworthiness and on how keen the Western capital markets are about doing business with this region.

International organizations

Funds from international organizations have been relatively new alternatives in East–West finance.[23] Hungary received a new IMF stand-by credit in May 1988, as mentioned in chapter 2. Romania's debt obligations to these institutions in the late 1980s amounted to 35 per cent of its total outstanding.[24] Poland had no access to the funds of these organizations during the 1980s. In early 1989 the World Bank stated that a series of loans to Poland running at a rate of about $250 million a year initially was to be expected. The Bank commitment could build up to more than $400 million a year for projects in agriculture, energy, transport and telecommunications (*The Financial Times*, 19 April 1989, p. 3). After the election of the Solidarity-led government in Poland in late 1989 discussions on new loans between Poland and the World Bank and the IMF were activated. Poland received the first IMF and World Bank credits in early 1990 (see p. 43).

The Soviet Union, Bulgaria and Czechoslovakia have made contact with the World Bank in the late 1980s and membership of both was advocated for the GDR by a former secretary of its Central Committee, Werner Felke (*The Financial Times*, 3 October 1988, p. 4). Bulgaria and Czechoslovakia applied to join the Bretton Woods institutions in early 1990. The Soviet Union announced in 1988 that it had established 'working contacts' with the Bank and the IMF (*The Financial Times*, 23 June 1988, p. 2). Academician Aganbegyan stressed in the presentation in London already referred to that his country will apply to join the two organizations as a part of the new Soviet policy to participate in the major world trade and financial organizations (GATT, World Bank, IMF and BIS). The Soviet Union has joined the International Asian Development Bank, the European Bank for Reconstruction and Development, and its participation in the International African Bank is under consideration. However, it would be too optimistic to expect that the Soviet Union will join the World Bank and the IMF in the short term. The main issues of Soviet participation must obviously be negotiated and discussed with the United States, the holder of the main shares in the World Bank and the IMF and the biggest Western trading nation. In early 1989 academician Aganbegyan stated in a conference in New York that he was optimistic about the prospect of the Soviet Union joining the IMF, the World Bank and GATT and did not have 'any doubts about the necessity of being a member of these organizations'. He stressed further that 'we are ready to begin nego- tiations but it will not be an easy process. It not only depends on us, but on the attitude of leading Western countries, and most of all the United States' (*The Financial Times*, 4 April 1989, p. 2). It is realistic to expect that the Soviet Union will first join GATT before the inter- national financial institutions during the 1990s. The smaller Eastern European countries, Bulgaria and Czechoslovakia, are pursuing a policy of joining the international financial institutions in the early 1990s given the changes in Soviet policy towards these organizations and the announced policy of the Soviet Union not to intervene in internal economic and political issues of the individual CMEA coun- tries. It is expected that the IMF and the World Bank will considerably increase their lending in Eastern Europe in order to support market- oriented economic reforms and the democratisation process in these countries.

Eastern European access to the international securities markets

A final field for increased Eastern European activity is on international security markets. Since the beginning of the 1980s inter- national financial markets have been undergoing major operational changes with 'securitization' being the most innovative trend. Finan- cial intermediation is channelled to a large extent through the issue and purchase of marketable securities rather than by the banking mechanism of lending and deposit-taking.

The international securities markets developed as markets for high quality borrowers (primarily from the industrialized countries). The debt servicing difficulties of the developing countries[25] and Eastern European countries in the early 1980s have limited (or precluded) their access to the market. Only a few developing countries (mainly East Asian countries – Malaysia, Hong Kong, Singapore, Thailand

Table 12   *Eastern Europe's securities offerings, 1984–1988 (billions of US dollars)*

	1984	1985	1986	1987	1988 (Jan.–Sept.)	1988 (Total)
Hungary						
External bond offerings	0.04	0.4	0.3	0.5	0.5	0.56
Floating rate issues		0.3	0.1	0.015		
Note issuance facilities	0.085	0.1				
Soviet Union						
External bond offerings				0.06	0.264	0.264
Czechoslovakia						
External bond offerings					0.075	0.07
Floating rate issues					0.05	0.05

Source: OECD, *Financial Market Trends*, no. 41, November 1988, p. 88, 90; no. 42, 1989, p. 39; BIS, *International Banking and Financial Market Developments*, Basle, December 1988, p. 38.

and China) were able to tap the international bond, floating rate note, note issuance facilities markets and the secondary market for resale of debt.

Among the Eastern European countries only Hungary, the Soviet Union and Czechoslovakia were present on the securities market in recent years. The Soviet Union placed its first three bond issues in 1987–9, as discussed in chapter 2. Hungary was able to tap the market for small amounts in 1984 and made larger borrowings in 1985–8. Czechoslovakia tapped the market in 1988 (bond issues and floating rate notes). Table 12 presents Eastern Europe's securities offerings in 1984–8.

The main source of borrowings were external bond offerings. They increased from $40 million in 1984 to $560 million in 1987 and $900 million in 1988. The floating rate issues and the note issuance facilities were represented by small amounts in 1984–8. In 1989 Hungary again tapped the bond market and had consultations with West German and US authorities regarding the expansion of the activities of Hungarian banks issuing and placing bonds on the Western financial markets (*The Financial Times*, 3 August 1989, p. 2).

The Eastern European countries with relatively good credit standing will be able in the future to borrow on the international securities markets. However, these countries still do not have the necessary experience. Poland will probably be excluded because the market remains a 'low risk borrowers' market. Access for Hungary might be restricted in the future because of the deterioration of its external balance of payments. The same refers to the other Eastern European countries.

In general, Eastern Europe, like most of the developing countries, will continue to be dependent on bank loans (to the extent that they are available) and official sources of credit in the years to come. However, the CMEA countries (particularly the Soviet Union, Hungary and Poland) will be interested in having access to international bond markets because of the potential advantages in terms of fixed interest rates and longer maturities of bonds over bank loans as a source of long-term capital flows.

4 Medium- and long-term debt prospects in Eastern Europe

The Eastern European countries liberalised their trade and credit relations with the West in the early 1970s, the first period of detente in East–West relations. During one decade they contracted a massive debt to the West and in 1981 Poland and Romania announced their inability to service the external debt, and Hungary and the GDR experienced a serious liquidity crisis. Bulgaria also experienced liquidity difficulties in 1978–9. The accumulation of debt continued during the 1980s. The question arises whether the convertible currency debt will be inherent in the economic development of Eastern Europe in the next decade, considered to be the second period of detente in East–West relations? This chapter discusses the impact of the economic reforms on the CMEA external balance and creditworthiness and likely developments in the medium and long term.

Economic reform and the external balance

The Hungarian economist B. Csikos-Nagy remarked more than fifteen years ago (1974) that a 'deficit balance of the Eastern European nations seems to be a constant phenomenon of the East–West economic relations'.[1] Will this statement be valid also in the 1990s?

Foreign borrowing can be considered as a trade across time, for external financial problems cannot be solved without trade. On the other hand debt servicing capacity must be judged on long-term economic growth prospects rather than on a net debt level. The international borrowing and repayment of debt of the Eastern European countries is related to a two-gap problem: the first gap is the savings-investment gap (that between income produced and income absorbed; the increase in foreign borrowing when income absorbed exceeds income produced) and the second gap is that between current account payments and receipts. A country cannot solve the transfer problem[2] without a long and difficult adjustment in economic policy towards a development strategy which increases the efficiency of production and the creation of an industrial base that is competitive by world market standards.

In 1987 to 1989 the Eastern European countries (other than Romania and the GDR) announced the introduction and implementation of radical reforms in their economic mechanism (see chapter 1). Gorbachev stressed in many speeches the need to 'intensify' the whole economy *inter alia* by the introduction of the most advanced technical and technological achievements. The Hungarian leadership declared a policy of increased production on the basis of the most advanced technology and thereby on the potential for faster economic development. A. Aganbegyan wrote that the restructuring process under way in the Soviet Union was 'real and not cosmetic and it will move forward'.[3]

To consider whether economic reforms would contribute to the abatement of convertible-currency debt problems, a survey of Eastern European reform is in order.

At the national level

1 reducing the role of central planning and increasing the autonomy of the enterprise;
2 increasing the importance of prices determined by 'market' relations, and phasing out administrative pricing;
3 strengthening the role of the banking and financial system;
4 dismantling the monopoly of the Ministry of Foreign Trade or its equivalent agency by according a large number of firms foreign trading rights;
5 allowing private activity in many sectors (particularly small-scale services);
6 introduction of convertibility of the national currency as a long-term goal.

At the regional level

1 applying the market to intra-CMEA trade;
2 effecting the convertibility of Comecon international currency, the transferable rouble (TR).

The reforms require fundamental changes in the general management and planning system which although it might be successfully introduced in the short term (as in Poland in 1990) might prove difficult to sustain in the medium term; considerable shifts are required in resource allocation at the sectoral, branch and regional levels and in income policy. The immediate aims of the reforms in Eastern Europe are more likely to be concentrated on increasing discipline, dismissing inefficient workers and increasing financial incentives to meet the targets of the government. The achievement of the long-run goals will also depend on factors beyond the control of the Eastern European countries, notably the international political and economic atmosphere.

The three principal components of the current account – exports, imports and interest payments – are in the short term determined largely by external factors of which six must be considered as adversely affecting the external balance of the Eastern European countries:

1 the widening technological gap between East and West;
2 prospects for relatively weak economic growth (2–2.5 per cent real GNP growth) and high unemployment in the market economies in the early 1990s and the probability of a recession;
3 serious competition by the newly industrialized countries (notably Brazil, Argentina, Mexico, Hong Kong, Taiwan, and Singapore) in manufactures (electro-mechanical equipment, iron and steel, ship-building, petrochemicals, and light industry products);
4 protectionism in Western Europe, the United States and Japan;
5 deterioration in Eastern Europe's terms of trade attributable to falling oil, gas, coal prices;
6 the expectation of a further rise in interest rates.[4] It should be considered here also that the German reunification will probably lead to an increased credit demand in Germany which would result in a rise of world market interest rates.

These influences indicate that over the short and medium term the economic reforms will have little impact on the abatement of the Eastern European external debt problem. But the prospects in the long term are also poor.

The economic reforms are in their 'embryonic' period at present. The programmes for economic liberalization in Poland and Hungary were strongly advanced in late 1989 but it would be too optimistic to expect that these programmes will be successfully implemented soon after they are introduced. The economic reforms will not change *de facto* the logic of the economic system and remove all centrally planned controls and restrictions of Eastern Europe (particularly in the Soviet Union, Bulgaria and Czechoslovakia) in the medium term. Although there are considerable shifts towards democratic societies (particularly the developments of late 1989 and early 1990 in Bulgaria, Czechoslovakia, the GDR and Romania), the economic reforms still are not based on a *fundamental* political liberalization in the East European political systems (except for Poland and Hungary to a certain extent which demonstrated in late 1989 their determination to become multiparty democratic societies in the medium term). However, the elections in Hungary in early 1990 showed that the population support for the reform changes was still weak; less than 50 per cent of the population eligible to vote participated in the elections. On the macroeconomic level there is little evidence that Eastern Europe will be able (even after the mid-1990s) to implement an effective expenditure reduction (by fiscal, monetary or income policies) and an expenditure switching (affecting the relative price of internationally tradable goods by exchange rates, tariffs and export promoting policies). The successful long-term switching of domestic output would require the existence of real market and market-oriented monetary, fiscal, income and exchange rate policies.[5] The creditworthiness of the Eastern European countries in the long term will depend crucially on the sensitivity of domestic to world prices through a reformed price mechanism, realistic exchange rates, utilization of capital markets, realistic interest rates, policies oriented at improving the profitability of investment, the enforcement of structural changes through competitive institutions (banks, etc.), market-oriented tax and tariff policies, policies to attract foreign investments and thus expand the productive base of the domestic economy. Poland and Hungary are likely to be the first Eastern European countries in which by the end of the 1990s market-oriented policies rather than 'direct controls' will probably be the response to external disturbances if the present programmes for economic liberalization are successfully implemented. One might also speculate on whether Czechoslovakia will be successful in achieving similar economic goals during the 1990s. I would like to suggest an optimistic answer given its old historic and cultural traditions and close links to Western Europe.

The reforms in all of the Eastern European countries are not part of a long-term plan for institutional changes, in the sense of a blue-print for the system to be created in the end, associated with a long-term plan for economic policy. An important point is that (even in Poland, Hungary and the Soviet Union) the various groups and individuals of the policy-making elite have rather differing visions of the future; the reform process at present and in the future requires not only a collection of 'radical' new laws and good rules for economic management, but people – decision makers, officials and managers – who have adjusted to these new rules.

There is little evidence that the present economic reforms could resolve by the mid-1990s the major difficulties in foreign trade relations, notably commodity non-convertibility, currency non-convertibility (for both national currencies and the transferable rouble), the inability to use devaluation (even in Hungary) as an instrument for achieving a trade balance, and bilateralism in intra-CMEA trade, i.e. to resolve some of the main problems of Eastern Europe that have led to the deficit-balance phenomenon in East–West trade. As regards currency convertibility it is worth noting the statement of the Hungarian banker J. Fekete, made in 1978, that 'convertibility in the Western sense would introduce such spontaneous elements into our planned economies which we cannot undertake'.[6] Convertibility will be a consequence of the creation of a market in the Eastern European countries (as discussed in chapter 1). There is also no evidence that price signals transmitted by the market in the reforming Eastern European economies reach the recipients with as little distortion as possible. The discussions on price reforms at present are rather on price formulas than on market clearing prices. It must be stressed also that liberalisation and stabilisation of the external sector, particularly for heavily indebted countries such as Poland and Hungary, cannot take place efficiently at the same time.

In the light of the modest prospects for Eastern European exports, financing will remain important (particularly for technological imports). But the imports of Western technology in the 1990s will not remove the main obstacles[7] to selling manufactured goods in competitive Western markets, notably comparative disadvantages in innovation, technological change, and marketing.[8] Even if Hungary, Poland and some other Eastern European countries become members of EFTA or receive an affiliation status with the European Community their exports to these regions will not be considerably boosted without successful market reforms and structural adjustment, a long and difficult process. The trade problems with the Western countries could prove to be the Achilles' heel of the adjustment policies of Eastern Europe in the 1990s.[9]

Eastern Europe could achieve a smoother transformation towards market economies and integration with the West if East-West political relations are stable and favourable and Eastern Europe receives substantial economic assistance from the West, e.g. if some sort of 'Economic Recovery Programme' for these countries were adopted, debt relief measures were applied and associations with the EC, or even the creation of a clearing union with some of the Western countries for multilateral trade and payments settlements were established (Zloch-Christy, 1990). Given the traditional contacts with Europe and a highly skilful population, Eastern Europe would have the potential under such circumstances for a development strategy which might lead to the creation by the end of this decade of a group of the 'newly industrialised countries' in Central and Eastern Europe. I would call such a scenario an 'optimistic scenario'. Obviously it is difficult to speculate on such outcomes.

How to assess the effects of the reform changes?

The ongoing market-oriented economic reforms in Eastern Europe are aimed at changing priorities and economic policy. The question arises of how to measure the effects of changes, in the sense of how successful is the introduction and the implementation of the reform measures? This section does not attempt to provide specific answers to this difficult question, but rather to establish a basis for a better understanding of the direction in which the reform process and economic development in Eastern European countries can be expected to move.

The central measures by which macroeconomic performance in every country (market economy, centrally planned economy, mixed economy) is judged are GNP, employment, inflation, and net exports. The main objectives of macroeconomic policies are high level and rapid growth rate of output, high level of employment, price level stability, export and import equilibrium and exchange rate stability. The instruments used in implementing macroeconomic policies in market economies usually include fiscal, monetary, income, trade and exchange rate policies. But the above mentioned policies and instruments have different economic effects in the centrally planned economies.[10] As a starting point for assessing changes in macroeconomic policies in the reform-oriented Eastern European countries obviously it is necessary to analyse in Western economic terms what instruments these countries apply in order to achieve the above mentioned main objectives of economic policy, in other words, what is the impact of domestic fiscal, monetary, income, trade, and exchange rate policies on the macroeconomic performance, the allocation of resources and the adjustment to external disturbances? Do the Eastern European countries continue to rely on policies of 'direct control',[11] or on market-oriented policies and instruments? Some of the interesting questions in this regard are: how does the system for allocation of capital 'work'? what is the role of interest rates? how does the allocation of foreign exchange in the economy occur? what is the role of the banking system in the economy? what are the changes in the price system? how many new enterprises were created? what is the role of the bureaucracy in economic decision making: what targets are they pursuing and how they are trying to achieve them? and many others.

The economic reform process in Eastern Europe is in its embryonic form (chapter 1 and p. 79). It is difficult to say where changes in macroeconomic policies should begin. The transformation from centrally planned economies to market-oriented/or market economies will obviously be long. How long? It is difficult to give a clear-cut answer to this question. But it seems reasonable to assume that at least the first half of the 1990s will be a transition period. In the author's view the following basic changes are required in the transition period:

1 import liberalizations;
2 market clearing prices;
3 unified exchange rates and convertibility on the current account; and
4 eliminating of direct and indirect state subsidies.

Associated with these basic changes is, of course, the expectation that the market-oriented economic reforms will be closely linked with the political liberalization of the Eastern European societies and with a diminution in the role of the communist party and bureaucracy in the management of the economy.[12] In other words, using the definition of the Hungarian economist and Harvard professor, J. Kornai, the reform process should be associated with 'any change in the economic system, provided that it diminishes the role of bureaucratic coordination and increases the role of market'.[13] The successful introduction and implementation of the economic reforms could be analysed by assessing to what extent, in practice, radical changes in ownership, incentives, the correction of informal 'rules of the game' (which complement, hinder, or enforce government resolutions and legal regulation) etc. are taking place.

The analysis on the microeconomic level should concentrate on the following objectives: autonomy of the enterprises; accountability of the enterprises for profit and loss; personal profit motivation of the enterprises' employees; and enterprises' efficiency (as compared to the pre-reform period).

The accountability of the enterprises for profit and loss is one of the most important indicators for the successful implementation of a market-oriented economic reform in the bureaucratic Eastern European economic systems since it gives an answer to the following two fundamental questions: firstly, do the enterprises operate on the basis of 'hard' or 'soft' budget constraints?[14], and secondly, to what extent firms' profits depend on bureaucratic intervention (direct corrections of prices, taxes, subsidies, etc.)[15]

Another important criterion for the success of the reform process is the evidence of positive correlation between enterprise efficiency, investments and future profits. In market economies the resource allocation is regulated by the market, profit being the main driving force; the major economic forces that determine investments are: the revenues, the cost of investment (determined by interest rates and tax policy), and the state of expectations about the future. In the planned economies of Eastern Europe, the party and the state bureaucracy often ignore (or miscalculate) profit as a resource allocation criterion which resulted in many inefficient investments over the last more than forty years.

An analysis of the correlation between profit and the personal income of the enterprise's workers indirectly answers the question if the workers have a personal interest in profit and thus in improving the efficiency of the enterprise. A market-oriented economic reform is expected to increase the interest of workers in a firm's profit – higher level of profit should be associated with higher level of personal income and less state regulations for the level of wages and salaries.

This brief discussion on the approaches to assessing the effects of changes as a result of the market-oriented reform process in Eastern Europe undoubtedly raises as many questions as it answers. At the same time, it establishes a basis for an analysis of present and future economic development in Eastern Europe, and its fundamental problem – market versus central planning.

Political risk assessment in lending to Eastern Europe

The debt problems of Eastern Europe and the economic reforms in most of these countries in the second half of the 1980s have greatly increased the interest shown by commercial banks, investment banks, government agencies, international institutions and business firms in evaluating risk.[16] Eastern Europe was regarded by Western business and financial circles in the previous more than three decades as a region with a stable political structure – totalitarian communist states. This fact determined the underestimation of the significance of political risk assessment. The new *perestroika* policy in the Soviet

Union and in most of the other Eastern European countries since the mid-1980s, and the policy changes in late 1989 in Romania and the GDR, raise the problem for evaluating *perestroika* risk in the region, considered to be in a dramatic time of change in the economic, political and social spheres. A political risk assessment in doing business with Eastern Europe should be an integral part of any international port-folio management process. It should accompany the analysis of the individual Eastern European countries' liquidity and structural prob-lems (debt service ratio, international reserves, delayed payments and arrears, rate of growth of GNP/GDP, hard-currency exports relative to GNP/GDP, composition of intra-CMEA trade in clearing currency, and many others).

This section attempts to provide an analytical framework for a discussion of approaches to the evaluating of political and social risk in doing business with Eastern Europe. The emphasis is on the questions and not on the answers.

Country risk is exposure to a loss in cross-border lending caused by events in a particular country and involves both economic and political risk. The conventional wisdom in lending to Eastern Europe has been that the risk to lenders is always a *country* risk problem rather than a *project* risk problem. In market economies normal lending risks are project risks, unless and until the whole nation experiences an economic management and external payments crisis. In Eastern Europe, most projects (in Romania all projects) are contracted with state organizations; the individual CMEA country will meet its debt obligations even if the specific project fails. Thus, in lending to Eastern Europe the sovereign, country, and project risks tend to be viewed as one and the same.

This concept of country risk analysis is still valid today. However, the present economic reforms in the Soviet Union and four other CMEA countries – Poland, Hungary, Bulgaria and Czechoslovakia – have increased the autonomy of domestic enterprises and created the possibility for them to have direct access to the Western markets. In some of these countries – the Soviet Union, Hungary, Poland and Bulgaria – domestic firms, banks, and branch ministries are allowed to raise funds on the international capital markets. These changes increase the importance of evaluating political and social risks in lending to Eastern Europe.

Political risks in lending across national borders are those generated by political entities beyond one's national jurisdiction. The study of political risks in doing business with Eastern Europe is the study of national and international political processes that can influence the level of risk involved in the undertakings of some Western entity operating in an environment sufficiently influenced by political factors which cannot be ignored. The political risks are associated with sociopolitical upheavals, willingness of the authorities to meet foreign debt obligations and many others. These risks are essentially dynamic and uncertain and are not easy to assess.

There are two key aspects of political risk in relation to country risks in lending to Eastern Europe:

1 interactions between domestic economic policy and political developments;
2 interactions between political developments, foreign confidence and capital inflows.

Starting from these points the analysis of political risks in lending to Eastern Europe requires an answer to four fundamental questions. Firstly, what is the country's leadership and its determination in carrying out economic political reforms? Second, what are the social conditions in the country and does social support exist for government policies? Third, what is the influence of the Soviet Union on a particular country's domestic political developments and can Soviet assistance be expected in case of economic difficulties? Fourth, what is the state of East–West political relations?

A key starting point of political risk assessment is an evaluation of a country's leadership. This evaluation may illuminate the prospects for the success and continuity of the country's political developments (*perestroika*, democratisation, openness), as well as its economic management. A Western businessman contemplating establishing a joint venture, for example in the Baltic republics, or in Georgia, in the Soviet Union, is keenly interested to know what are the prospects for *perestroika* and independence in the medium and long term. A Western banker considering a provision of credit to a Soviet enterprise is also confronted with this basic question. In late 1988, the Estonian reformers announced a radical package of reforms including, among others, proposals for an Estonian currency and regional development policies based largely on external borrowings; it was proposed that some $10.0 billion be raised on the international capital markets (*The Financial Times*, 1 December 1988, p. 1). The first question to be asked by Western businessmen providing loans to an Estonian entity obviously would be how one could be sure that a particular enterprise or a bank in Estonia would repay the debt in five years time? The same question arises in lending to Polish, Hungarian or Bulgarian entities.

However, although all of the above mentioned Eastern European countries belong to the same political and economic community of the Council for Mutual Economic Assistance, there are in practice specific differences among them. No two of these countries are alike. Furthermore, obviously questions relevant for the Eastern European countries which carry out an economic *perestroika* policy at present will differ from those relevant for the countries – the GDR and Romania, which in late 1989 demonstrated their strong efforts towards democratisation, but did not undertake concrete steps in the direction of radical economic reforms. The reunification of the GDR and FRG, however, is a factor of great significance considering the changes in the GDR and the prospects for economic organisation there. What is important for the analyst is to understand the key developments in a particular Eastern European country and to know which questions to ask.

The most important question to be asked as regards the reform-oriented East European countries, and particularly the Soviet Union, is what are the chances that the countries' leaderships will succeed in implementing the plans for liberalisation of the economy and the associated plans for the political democratisation of the totalitarian Eastern European societies? If the economic reforms fail, the prognosis would obviously be economic and political instability in these countries and continued relative economic decline.

The following questions are interesting in evaluating a country's leadership. Does the leadership consist of reformers or of rather conservative party bureaucrats and 'apparatchiks'? What are the professional skills of the leadership? Does it support technocrats or not? Does it understand economics and what is the managerial background of the leadership? Associated with these questions are questions related to the political support of the leadership. Which groups support the party and government leadership? What is the basis of its control, e.g. popular support? What are the attitudes and roles of the various institutions – bureaucracy, military, etc.? How strong are the opposition groups? The next question to ask is what is the probability that the leadership will be changed and what is the most likely alternative leadership? Will the new leadership consist of the old conservative party guard, of the new opposition parties, or of extremist radical communist party reformers? In the case of the Soviet Union the question, for example, might be Ligachev (conservative) versus Yeltsin (extremist radical reformer)?

In the individual Eastern European countries there will be a specific issue or problem which needs to be examined, and then watched for future developments. For example, who will be the successors of the communist leaders who replaced the ageing dictators of Bulgaria, the GDR and Romania in late 1989? In the case of Romania, a further interesting question arises – will the new leader continue the path of the present unsophisticated economic and debt management (highly centralized planning system) or will it follow the path of radical *perestroika* policy?

Another country-specific question which needs to be highlighted and examined is whether there are ethnic or religious disturbances in the individual Eastern European countries. Almost all of these countries face potential unrest due to such disturbances. The latter could have a major impact on domestic politics (e.g. power struggle) and the economy–instability and, associated with that, declining production, exports, etc. Without going into details, the ethnic disturbances and movements towards independence in Georgia, Azerbaidjan, and the Baltic republics in the Soviet Union, as well as in Romania, Czechoslovakia and Bulgaria must be taken into account.

Another interesting question which arises in assessing political risk is whether foreign confidence exists in the economic and political developments in the individual Eastern European countries? Foreign confidence in the country's development and its leadership greatly affects the state of trade and credit relations between East and West. For example, the confidence of the Western countries in the policy of Hungary in the early 1980s led to its access to the IMF and the World Bank and to new capital inflows, which allowed debt reschedulings to be avoided. At the same time the unsophisticated economic and debt management of Poland and Romania determined an end to Western capital inflows and debt reschedulings then became unavoidable. The liberalization of political life in Poland in 1989 (legalising of Solidarity and the election of the Solidarity-led government) were the main factors which affected the change of Western attitudes towards Poland and the probability that it will receive credits from the IMF, the World Bank, new commercial bank loans, USA preferential export tariff treatment, more favourable conditions on reschedulings of the Paris Club, commercial bank credits, and others in the early 1990s.

The economic and political developments in the individual Eastern European countries can rarely be considered in isolation from regional and world events. The Eastern European countries are members of the CMEA. Although the integration processes in the region have faced

serious problems for more than four decades, and recent changes in
domestic policies in the CMEA countries, and in East–West relations,
suggest that the future belongs to the intensification of trade and
credit relations between Eastern Europe and the Western countries,
one might suggest that common cooperation plans might affect the
decision of a country's leadership regarding domestic economic
policy, or its determination to expand economic relations with the
Western countries (in general, or in a particular field, e.g. certain
production, banking, etc.). This indicates that main trends in CMEA
integration (pricing policy, cooperation agreements, and others)
should be examined. Some of the interesting questions to be asked are:
are there changes in the inter-CMEA pricing policy[17] and if so, how
will they affect the relations of the particular Eastern European
country with the CMEA members, developed Western nations and
developing countries; how the plans for convertibility of the CMEA
national currencies and of the integration currency, the transferable
rouble (TR), and their probable implementation in the 1990s will
influence the relationship of the CMEA with the rest of the world?

In the context of the influence of regional events on the economic
and political developments in the individual Eastern European countries, it is worth noting here that in the case of the GDR its 'special
relationship' with West Germany, and the reunification of the two
German states, should be carefully considered. An interesting question to be asked is, for example, how the 1992 policies of the European
Community (EC) will affect the economic development of East
Germany? How will the reunification of Germany affect economic life
and development strategies in East Germany? In the context of the
independence movements in the Baltic republics, an interesting question is what will be the affects of Moscow's economic measures
(cutting oil and gas deliveries) against the individual republics?
Another question is whether the Baltic republics will form an
economic integration community and how it will affect the independence movement in the region.

Political risk assessment also requires an analysis of the social
conditions in the individual Eastern European countries. Social tensions are less immediate in the sense that they are unlikely to apply,
for example, to export payments. However, they are particularly likely
to apply to long-term investment projects (joint ventures, cooperation
agreements, and others). The analysis of social conditions is a critical
part of a country risk evaluation, particularly for countries like the

Soviet Union, Poland and Hungary. The main question to be asked is: does strong social support for the government policies exist? The events in Poland in the 1970s and in the 1980s and the policies of the present Solidarity-led government suggest that an accurate assessment of the social tensions may be of urgent importance for Western bankers and businessmen. Social tensions can precipitate political crisis, change government priorities and policies and even change the leadership. In the case of the Soviet Union, a careful analysis of the influence of the policy of *perestroika* on the social conditions in this country is essential, since the improvement of social conditions and living standards will be of critical importance for the social support for Gorbachev's policies.

Political risk analysis also requires an assessment of the relations between the individual Eastern European countries and the Soviet Union. In the 1960s and 1970s the Western business and political circles regarded Eastern Europe as a region 'under the Soviet umbrella' which guarantees Soviet assistance in case of economic difficulties. The 'umbrella theory' was based on the expectation that the Soviet Union would assist its allies for prestigious and political reasons. The CMEA debt servicing problems (especially those of Poland, Hungary and Romania) have shown this to be false. Gorbachev's policies towards Eastern Europe at present indicate that it would be too optimistic to expect a 'Soviet umbrella' in future economic difficulties in the individual Eastern European countries. The statement made by Gorbachev in his discussion with the former Hungarian leader K. Grosz in early 1989, that the Soviet Union does not intend to intervene in domestic economic and political developments in the CMEA countries, was one of the first signals, followed by a clear Soviet position at present, not only for more political 'freedom' for Eastern Europe, but also for the necessity of the Soviet allies to rely on themselves more and not to expect Soviet assistance. However, there are country-specific differences in the relations between the Soviet Union and the individual Eastern European countries, which an analyst should follow.

It has to be stressed here that economic instability might arise in the Eastern Europe Six because of Soviet policies. All of these countries have strong economic and trade links with the Soviet Union and their economies can be influenced by the economic situation in the latter. An interesting question to be asked is, for example, what will be the policy of the Soviet Union as regards the rouble debts of its allies?

Lastly, the state of East–West political relations should be one of the most important parts of a political risk assessment for Eastern Europe. The East–West political dialogue determines economic, trade and credit policies in the individual Eastern European countries towards the West. There are many questions to be asked at present. What are the prospects for economic relations between CMEA and the European Community, given the 1992 European Community plans? Can one expect that some of the Eastern European countries will apply for an association status with the European Community, and what will be the effects on their domestic economic and political developments and on the relationships with the Soviet Union? What is the likelihood that the Soviet Union will join the international financial institutions (IMF and the World Bank)?

This section presented a set of questions the analyst should raise when exploring political risk in Eastern Europe. I briefly indicated my tentative answers as well, at least to some of the questions. I do hope that even if the analyst arrives at answers different to mine, my questions would be helpful to him in future studies.

Alternative scenarios

This chapter does not seek to project on the basis of a computer model the Eastern European convertible currency debt as I did recently (1986, 1988), but to discuss likely developments in global economic conditions both in Eastern Europe and in the West which will influence the CMEA external balance (trade balance, gross and net debt) in the next decade. Three main alternative scenarios are considered:

1 what would be the developments in hard-currency debt under the assumption that Eastern Europe pursues a policy of restricted imports, which remain fixed in real terms?
2 what would be the debt level if Eastern Europe increases Western imports and external borrowing?
3 what would be the debt level if CMEA countries increase Western imports and external borrowing but control the net debt level.

The analysis concentrates on likely developments in the economic conditions. The influence of uncertain political factors has not been considered. However, the future level of debt will be determined by a combination of changing economic and political factors.

The major economic determinants of outlook for Eastern European indebtedness in the 1990s are: First, the state of Soviet external borrowing and hence the level of its debt will be determined to a lesser extent by Soviet planners than in the past but rather by the availability of Western credits. Thus, not only developments in the domestic economy will determine external borrowing but tensions in the external balance may lead to increased shortages in the domestic economy. This implies that access by the Soviet Union to the Western capital markets will depend on a combination of demand and supply factors (availability of credits) with the latter becoming increasingly important. This applies to Czechoslovakia as well.

Secondly, in the case of Hungary and Poland the supply of credit by Western banks, government agencies and exporters will determine the level of convertible-currency balance of payments and current account and thus also the required level of trade balance. This situation is likely to persist for both countries during the 1990s. Hungary and Poland have to make further appropriate macro-economic adjustments in their economies so as to satisfy the external balance constraints (even in the case of successful negotiations for debt reduction).

Thirdly, in the case of Bulgaria, Romania and the GDR (until the reunification of Germany), the level of external debt continues to be determined mainly by demand factors but the supply of Western credits will have an important impact as well. This implies that developments in the domestic economies of these countries will be constrained by the external balance. This applies very strongly to Bulgaria, which rapidly accumulated convertible-currency debt in 1986–88.

Ten other key factors will determine the outlook for East–West trade and CMEA external debt in the next decade:

1 demand for Eastern European exports in the West and in the developing countries;
2 Eastern European terms of trade with the rest of the world (developments in oil, gas, coal, and manufacturing prices);
3 level of interest rates;
4 stand-by agreements and access to the funds of the international financial organisations (IMF and the World Bank);
5 adjustments in intra-CMEA trade policy;
6 Eastern European borrowing policy;
7 developments in the rouble debts of the Eastern European countries to the Soviet Union;
8 the role that Western machinery could play in the re-tooling of the Eastern European industry;
9 in the relationship between Eastern and Western Europe, the

success of the negotiations between the EC and the individual CMEA countries and probable affiliation for membership for some of the Eastern European countries in the EC and EFTA;

10 Western debt relief measures applied to Eastern Europe (possibly to Poland and Hungary).

The likely impact of some of these key factors (Western demand, terms of trade, interest rates, CMEA borrowing policy) were discussed in chapters 2 and 4 (p. 79). As regards developments in energy prices, it is very important to analyse further their impact on Western demand for Eastern European goods in the medium term. The recent rise in oil prices is likely to continue. However, the peak levels of the late 1970s and early 1980s will probably not be reached. The rising oil prices might adversely affect economic activity in the OECD countries and in oil-consuming developing countries. This, in turn, will lead to a decrease in the growth of demand for imports, especially imports of manufactured goods and primary raw materials. Rising energy prices might lead to further rises in world market interest rates. All that (not to forget the competition from developing countries) indicates that the demand for Eastern European exports will decrease and the cost of servicing debt will increase in the short and medium term.

At the same time the prices of most non-fuel commodities (including agricultural products) will continue to remain rather stagnant. The suppliers of these commodities are increasing their exports as a consequence of balance of payments pressures, while the demand is likely to expand rather slowly. Further constraints on Eastern European exports to the West will be the increased protectionist barriers particularly in the European Community and in the United States. According to an IMF analysis 'non-tariff measures have proliferated and possibly offset the effects of postwar reductions in tariffs. In the latter respect, the recent sharp increase in voluntary export restraints and similar arrangements has intensified restrictions in sectors, such as textiles, clothing and agriculture, that are already subject to quantitative restrictions' (World Economic Outlook, October 1988, p. 36). Among the Eastern European countries, Poland, Hungary and Czechoslovakia will benefit greatly from the provision of the most favoured nation status in their trade with the USA. The agreements with the European Community and the EC aid packages for Poland and Hungary would also contribute to their increased chance for an access to the markets in Western Europe.

If the oil prices continue to rise or stabilise at about $20.0 per barrel, the overall export revenues of Eastern Europe, which was a net exporter of energy for convertible currency (with the exception of Romania) in the 1970s and 1980s, might increase and thus offset to some point the adverse effect of the trends discussed above. Soviet energy production and exports (about 60 per cent of this is likely to be in oil) will continue to grow but at relatively lower rates than in the 1970s and in the first half of the 1980s. It is difficult to give a clear-cut answer to the question of how much the Soviet oil exports will grow, given almost stagnant output in late 1980s and the prospects for increasing domestic use certain to develop in the Soviet economy in the short and medium term as a result of economic reform.

Exports of arms to developing countries and particularly to major trading Middle Eastern partners – Iraq, Iran, Syria – and Libya, are expected to decline, because of the end of the Iran–Iraq war and because of the low level of reserves in these countries; the latter will require cuts in imports. The rising oil prices and revenues for these oil-exporting developing countries will not considerably influence their imports from Eastern Europe in the short and medium term (as in the 1970s and in the first half of 1980s). However, if the Soviet Union and the other Eastern European countries continue to reschedule the Middle Eastern countries' and Libya's debts (as in the case of Syria) a slight increase of Eastern European exports might be expected (*The Financial Times*, 28 March 1989: p. 2). It is important to note for all developing countries that even slow economic recovery in the Middle East, Africa, Latin America and South and South-East Asia (India and others) would have little affect on Eastern Europe's exports to the Third World in the short and medium term.

As regards Eastern European imports from the West and developing countries, one might expect an increase in their levels in the medium and long term given the plans for *perestroika* and modernisation of the economy in the reforming countries, and the long austerity period in the case of Romania. There is little doubt that huge demand for imports from the Western industrialised countries currently exists in Eastern Europe. This leads us to believe that Eastern Europe will increase imports in the short term rather than voluntarily compressing external indebtedness for non-economic reasons (as in the case of Romania in the 1980s). The growth of imports will be constrained at some point by the export revenues, but the anticipated availability of Western credits would partly offset the adverse effect of the latter. As regards the imports from developing countries, one might expect that they will rapidly increase in the short and medium term given the continued Eastern European need for grain and food imports (bad harvests in Eastern Europe in 1988–9; expected increase of consumption goods imports in the Soviet Union) as well as for certain raw materials.

Other key factors which will determine the outlook for the Eastern European convertible-currency debt are the developments in the rouble debts to the Soviet Union. The Eastern Europe Six (with the exception of Romania) is a net oil importing region from the Soviet Union. However, it did not benefit in 1985–9 from falling oil prices, due to the fact that most of Eastern Europe's imports (including energy products) are priced according to a moving five-year average of world prices; the price impact may be felt only gradually. At present the Eastern European Six have to export more to the Soviet Union in return for the same quality of Soviet deliveries. Some of the CMEA goods exported to the Soviet market, however, may be exported to the West, thus reducing the tension of the external balance of the former. This trend in intra-CMEA trade is likely to continue until the early 1990s. The falling Soviet oil revenues in recent years and the huge demand for Western imports forced the Soviet Union to divert oil from Eastern Europe to Western markets, offering Eastern Europe Six increased supplies of natural gas as a substitute. All that adversely affects the CMEA Six exports (and oil re-exports) to the West at present and in the short and medium term. However, if the moving intra-CMEA price formula remains unchanged, one might expect that from the early 1990s the Eastern European Six would have favourable terms of trade and would benefit from their oil trade with the Soviet Union. One should note here, that the Soviet Union will increase its (more stringent) quality requirements on CMEA Six exports to the Soviet market (effectively lowering the price of CMEA Six exports). This could become an important constraint on the ability of the East European Six to expand exports to the West.

As regards the repayment of rouble debts to the Soviet Union, it is not clear that Soviet strategy will continue to be avoidance of the risk of deepening the economic crisis in the region and pressing the Eastern European Six to rapidly repay their rouble debts. One might expect, however, that it will reschedule the repayments of the Polish rouble debt in the early 1990s. The Soviet Union realises the importance of the CMEA Six's ability to increase exports to the West, thus maintaining satisfactory trade balances and retaining access to Western financial markets. It will continue, however, to insist on repaying rouble debts on schedule (with the probable exception in the case of Poland in the early 1990s) and on increased quality requirements in the short and medium term. However, if in the early and mid-1990s Soviet economic performance and export revenues deteriorate, which is a very probable scenario given the unstable and uncertain Soviet political situation, there is a possibility that the Soviet Union will insist on a more rapid pace of rouble debt repayment or other major alterations in regional trade that would lead to reductions in Soviet exports to CMEA and reductions of CMEA Six exports to the West, which would increase the need of the CMEA Six for additional Western financing. The Soviet Union will probably increase, in the early 1990s, the requirements part of its trade with the CMEA Six to be settled in convertible currencies. This might lead to a rapid deterioration of the convertible-currency balances of the Eastern Europe Six with the Soviet Union, given that they import most of their oil, gas, and other raw materials from the Soviet Union. Some estimates suggest that, for example, Hungary will incur at least a $1 billion trade deficit with the Soviet Union in the short term, if more than 10 per cent of the Hungarian trade with the latter were to be settled in US dollars in the early 1990s (*The Economist*, 21 October 1989, p. 79).

During the first half of the 1990s (the new five-year plan period), the Soviet Union and most of the Eastern European countries are expected to re-tool their industrial capacity. This policy to modernise their capital stock could have a major impact on the region's trade with the West. A higher priority is likely to be assigned to imports of Western machinery and equipment. Much of the existing industrial capital stock already in place in the Soviet Union and Eastern Europe Six is based on Western equipment and technology, and in the effort to modernise their plant and equipment it is probably most cost-effective for them to return to the original suppliers for assistance. However, the Western restrictions on the flow of military-relevant high technology and the numerous past failures of imported equipment to achieve expected levels of productivity might be a certain constraint to rapidly increased Western imports, as during the 1970s. Some of the Eastern European countries (most likely Romania) will continue to be determined to produce domestic substitutes using their own or CMEA technology.

The recent negotiations and achieved trade agreements between the European Community and the individual Eastern European countries might lead to an increase in trade turnover in the medium term as a result of certain reductions of trade barriers between the two regions. The Eastern European imports of machinery and equipment will possibly increase. There would likely be some rise in the European Community's imports from the CMEA region as well.

The access to funds of the international financial organisations (IMF and the World Bank) and the success of the negotiated stand-by and adjustment agreements will remain essential for the creditworthiness of Poland and Hungary and probably for Bulgaria and Czechoslovakia in the 1990s. In the case of Romania, one might expect that after almost ten years of austerity policy it will return to the international capital markets in order to finance capital goods imports in the early 1990s. Improved relations with the international financial institutions will be very important for its access to commercial banks and government agencies' credits.

The Western debt relief measures for developing countries being discussed at present might be applied to some of the Eastern European countries (Poland and Hungary) as well. In the short and medium term this will lead to increased Western imports in these particular countries and to a certain reduction of their net new borrowings. It is not clear, however, if they will be able to stabilise their external sector in the long term, given the experience of the 1970s and the lack of evidence that the economic reforms will achieve radical changes in the efficiency of their economies in the medium term. If proposals for debt reduction, Japanese guaranteed debt-equity swaps (*The Financial Times*, 17 March 1989, p. 4) and debt deals like the Mexican deals for debt buy-backs will be applied to Poland and Hungary and other East European countries depends very much on political considerations. There are arguments that debt buy-backs are controversial.[18] However, Polish economists strongly support the idea for the debt buy-backs and are against debt-equity swaps.[19] Hungarian economists doubt also the debt relief brought by debt-equity swaps. Some Western scholars are, however, more favourable to the latter in the Eastern European context than for most indebted developing countries because of the tightly structured CMEA monetary system.[20] The plans for privatisation in Poland and Hungary offer good possibilities for debt/equity swaps. One might expect that the latter will have an application in debt relief programmes with the western creditors in the early 1990s (given a clearly defined East European strategy for foreign investments in their domestic economies). These debt relief measures would probably not be considered in the case of the other Eastern European countries in the short term.

The analysis of the debt developments in recent years, in chapter 2, and the main economic determinants of East–West trade and finance (discussed above) in the future point to three main conclusions of the outcomes of the alternative scenarios.

First, under the scenario that the growth of Western imports is restricted, Eastern European debt problems ease considerably. However, debt will not be eliminated. The debt levels for Poland and Hungary remain high. Bulgaria's debt will remain at a relatively high level.

Second, under the scenarios of increased Western imports and borrowing (and even by controlling net debt levels) the external balance deteriorates rapidly for Poland, Hungary and Bulgaria. Reschedulings or refinancing will be necessary for these countries. Debt servicing would create no serious problems in Czechoslovakia, the GDR, Romania and the Soviet Union. However, the external debt of the Soviet Union and the GDR until German reunification will rapidly rise to relatively high levels and liquidity squeezes might occur.

Third, the likelihood of a debt crisis in Eastern Europe, considered as a region, in the 1990s seems to be increasing, but it could be avoided (given the access of these countries to the Western capital markets).

Bulgaria. It appears likely that its debt levels will remain high. There is no evidence that Bulgaria will or could mount any major convertible currency export drive in the short term. It will continue to borrow (given the access to the market) and diversify the borrowing instruments but the experience of the liquidity crisis of the late 1970s will make it relatively 'cautious'. Its future good standing with the Bretton Woods institutions would be important for its access to the Western capital markets and for its potential to avoid a serious debt crisis.

Czechoslovakia. The gross and net debt profile will remain sound given its conservative borrowing policy. One might expect it to be active on the securities markets. Czechoslovakia will make cautious moves in favour of increases in imports of Western technology to stem the decline in industrial competitivity. The deterioration of its terms of trade with the Soviet Union and the expected new economic development strategy in the early 1990s might lead to an increase in its borrowing in the West, and in the external debt levels.

GDR (until German reunification). Given the political and economic instability in the country and the huge domestic budget deficit, it seems to be a difficult strategy for the GDR to keep the option of borrowing in the West only to the extent needed to support the plans for modernisation of its industry, which will require an influx of Western and especially West German investment goods (*The Financial Times*, 17 March 1989, p. 6). Debt will be manageable, but debt levels remain relatively high.

Hungary. The Hungarian external balance will cause serious concern for the domestic economy in the 1990s. Foreign debt will rise and the debt related indicators will be at 'alarming' levels. One might expect an increase of foreign investments in Hungary in early 1990, which will ease at some point the tension in the balance of payments. Policies to stem capital 'flight' seem to be necessary in the 1990s. Access to the Western capital markets will be crucial for the Hungarian creditworthiness.[21]

Poland. It will continue to face severe structural economic problems and an overwhelming debt burden if debt relief measures are not applied. Good relations with the international financial institutions, government agencies and commercial banks are a likely prospect in the short-term. As in the case of Hungary, this will be crucial for Polish creditworthiness in the next decade.[22] Some debt relief measures (debt repurchase at a certain discount, debt/bond swaps, debt/equity swaps, a reduced interest repayments/bond swaps, and certain varying discounts on debt) might be expected in early 1990. Western investors are interested in expanding business activities in Poland; after few years of stability in the implementation of the radical package for economic and political liberalisation (of late 1989) one might expect a rapid increase of foreign investments. The plans for privatisation might lead to large scale purchases of state-owned enterprises by Western firms; in late 1989 there were discussions between the Polish government, the Gdansk 'Lenin' shipyard and an US firm for purchasing the yard, the first deal of such scale between state-owned enterprise and Western firm (*The Financial Times*, 17 October 1989, p. 2). The expected some $4.5 billion (of which $3.0 billion to modernise Polish industry) new loans from Western countries in early 1990s indicate (IMF *Morning Press*, 26 October 1989) that the Solidarity-led government might pursue a growth-cum-debt policy in the short term which will lead to rapid accumulation of debt (even in case of debt reduction programmes). As in the case of Hungary, policies to stem capital 'flight' seem to be necessary in the short and medium term.

Romania. One might expect a retreat from the Romanian chosen path of completely isolation from the international financial community in its effort to repay debts as quickly as possible, in the early 1990s. Major borrowings, however, do not seem likely. However, there will certainly be a retreat from the unsophisticated economic and debt management of the Ceausescu government. The former Romanian dictator Ceausescu announced in early 1989 that 'we have decided not to depend on anyone anymore either economically or politically to really ensure the independence of our people, our nation' (*The Financial Times*, 17 April 1989, p. 2).

Soviet Union. An expected increase in Western investment goods imports will result in deterioration of the Soviet current account and a significant rise of borrowing and debt. The cooperation with Western firms (including joint ventures) will not offset this effect. The Soviet Union will pursue a policy towards de-ideologising its economic and credit relations with the other CMEA countries (including Vietnam, Cuba) and the military 'assistance' (arms exports) provided to developing countries, because of the past experience of liquidity difficulties and defaults of the developing countries on the repayment of such credits. The Soviet Union will be active on the international securities markets. However, unmanageable problems with its convertible-currency debt are not an unlikely scenario. The political and economic instability in the country will increase in the short term. The statement made by the Soviet prime minister in May 1990 that 'We have no more money. We have no more gold to buy grain', is a cause for serious concern (*The Financial Times*, 26/7 May 1990. p. 1). It is difficult to speculate whether Western countries will meet Soviet requirements for additional credits and aid measures given the complexity of the problems involved. An economic advisor to Gorbachev stressed, however, that 'without big credits from the West we will not be able to build the market economy ...' (*The Financial Times*, 29 May 1990, p. 1).

Conclusion

The analysis in the study indicates that it would be too optimistic to expect the Eastern European countries to pursue in the 1990s an outward-oriented development strategy based on export promotion and industrial base that is competitive by world market standards. It is rather that strategy the successful implementation of which seems to be the only way to improve permanently their convertible-currency external debt position in the future. Although Eastern Europe as a region has regained control over their external balances in the late 1980s a deficit balance of the Eastern European nations will remain a phenomenon of the East–West economic relations.

The economic reforms in most of the CMEA countries are radical in the sense that they attempt not only changing priorities and policies, but changing the economic system. But there are many uncertainties in the successful implementation of the reforms. The economic and political reforms still do not have a blue-print of the system to be achieved in the end, associated with a long-term plan for economic policy. Further more, the economic and political reforms are still not based on a fundamental political liberalisation in the Eastern European political structure (except in Poland and Hungary). Neither scholars and policy makers in Eastern Europe, nor Western scholars and politicians, have offered well demonstrated and irrefutable theorems for changing the nature of the CMEA socialist systems. As the prominent Hungarian economist J. Kornai pointed out, the study of socialist economies is not yet a mature discipline. 'Most of us, dealing with the subject, have only conjectures and hypotheses.'[1] All that indicates that the outcomes of the reforms will not be seen soon.

The economic reforms seem to be an important impetus for the liberalisation of the East-West economic relations and varifications of the forms of financing. Joint ventures, countertrade (counterpurchase and buy-backs), forfeiting, export-leasing, funds from international financial institutions, and borrowings in the international securities markets will develop further in the 1990s. The Soviet Union will apply to join the IMF, the World Bank, the regional development banks and GATT.

Given the political and economic instability in the region, it is difficult to remain optimistic (as in the late 1980s) and to expect that the debt problems of Eastern Europe as a region will be manageable in the short and medium term. However, debt crisis could be avoided given the access of these countries to the Western capital markets. The liquidity positions of Hungary and Poland will be crucially dependent on their access to Western capital. The solution to the external balance disequilibrium in these countries lies at the hands of their leaderships. The ability to pursue economic reform is very important in this regard. In all of the Eastern European countries substantial *de facto* modifications of the economic system and policies for structural adjustment, privatisation, for eliminating excess demand, improving supply elasticities, export performance and price structure, are urgently needed.

The policies of the Western creditor nations will also be very important for the restoration of growth in Poland and Hungary, and in the other East European countries. The proposals for debt relief to the major developing countries debtors, if applied to Poland and Hungary as well, would stimulate global growth and trade through an increased flow of financing into these countries (and the other countries in the region).

It is worth noting as a conclusion the statement made by Lord Keynes in the 1930s that the largest transfers of financial resources entailed by the proposed level of German war reparations would have a negative impact on the British economy for precisely the same reasons that transfers from developing countries and the major Eastern European debtor countries (Poland, Hungary) were damaging the world economy in the 1980s: 'We shall never be able to move again unless we free our limbs from these paper shackles. A general bonfire is so great a necessity that unless we can make of it an orderly and good-tempered affair in which no serious injustice is done to anyone, it will, when it comes at last, grow into a conflagration that may destroy much else as well'.[2]

Epilogue

The political and economic transformation of Eastern Europe in the 1990s is undoubtedly one of the important and interesting changes in the history of the old continent and of post-war world politics. Even the most conservative observers agree that the process is irreversible. Eastern Europe in the mid-1990s will be different from the same region in the mid-1980s dominated by Soviet influence, communist rule and centrally planned economies.

Eastern Europe is attempting to transform centrally planned economies into market or market-oriented economies, and democratizing their societies. This process is characterized by instability and unpredictability. The Soviet Union, the smaller Eastern European Five and East Germany (in unified Germany) are suffering from the growing pains of over-rapid changes, and from the painfulness of readjustment between the recent economic period and the new one. The major problems of this readjustment are the serious macroeconomic imbalances and the severe crises of confidence in the populations. The smaller Eastern European countries are confronted also with the necessity of clearly defining their economic development strategies in a rapidly changing political and economic environment. They all still lack a middle and long-term strategy for relations with the Soviet Union and within the CMEA on one hand, and for relations with the Western industrialized countries (and particularly with Western Europe) and the developing countries on the other hand. The Eastern European countries need to have a model and an alternative model of the economic reform. Another problem they are confronted with is the need to secure basic social welfare in order to maximize the economic programmes. The excess demand creates serious difficulties in implementing these programmes.

As Keynes (1963, p. 344) wrote more than half of century ago, 'the political problem of mankind is to combine three things: Economic

Efficiency, Social Justice and Individual Liberty'. This is the 'Herculean' task Eastern Europe is attempting to solve in the 1990s. The problem of choosing or deciding on an economic development policy in the individual Eastern European countries, or on what to do, can be approached by resolving it into answering and relating the answers to two questions, the positive-scientific-technical question 'what can be done'? and the ethical-political-evaluative question 'what should be done'? These questions cannot be answered in strictly economic theory terms but are questions more of political economy and politics. The answers in the individual Eastern European countries in the 1990s will be given with certainty by opportunity and preference judgements depending on specific national, political, economic, historic and cultural factors. The debate in the Soviet Union in late 1990 on a 'broader' or 'safer' policy (gradual changes) in discussions on the Shatalin/Aganbegyan programme for rapid transformation of the Soviet economy into a market economy in '500 days' and the 'gradual' programme of the Soviet prime minister, demonstrates clearly the enormous difficulties in defining the economic development strategies in Eastern Europe.

Eastern Europe has a potential for economic recovery given its traditional links with Western Europe and highly skilled population. Rational and pragmatic economic development strategies and their introduction at the 'right moment' without delay, combined with stable political and economic relations with the West, could provide the climate for the emergence of the group of new democracies in Central and Eastern Europe with its huge market, by mid-1990s or by the end of this decade. Obviously it is difficult to speculate on such outcomes and to do so would be only an intellectual exercise. But undoubtedly there is a potential for such development.

The innovative basis of market economies and the necessity of enlarging private ownership in the economic system are the main objectives of the reforms in Eastern Europe. At the same time it is realized by Eastern European politicians that in order to have the benefits of a market system these economies should live with partial government regulation. There is a need for a pragmatic attitude for such regulation and intervention in particular areas and in particular cases. The reforms also require time to 'taste' different forms of property in the economies of the individual Eastern European countries. Many questions arise in this connection: how to implement privatization without private capital? how to create stimulus for the economic agents? how to create the conditions for potential competition in order to diminish the power of the old monopolistic structures? how to attract foreign investors? and many others. The approach to these questions ('what can be done' or 'what should be done') will be not the same in each East European country. As was stressed earlier, it will depend on the specific political and economic goals of the governments and first of all on conditions in these countries and on the state of East–West relations. The art of political economy should determine the optimal approach to all these problems.

The economic development of Eastern Europe in the 1990s will depend on the inflow of foreign capital in the form of new loans and direct investments. The external debt burden of Eastern Europe, however, rapidly rose and reached more than \$150 billion and \$115 billion gross and net debt respectively in early 1990. Bulgaria suspended payments and reschedulings of her debt (as in the case of Poland) are unavoidable. The Soviet Union experienced liquidity difficulties. Hungary's access to the Western capital markets is associated with hardening of the borrowing conditions. Czechoslovakia and Romania experienced deterioration in their trade balances. The Western countries, considering the fact that the cold war period was so expensive, continued to demonstrate their support for the economic and political transformation in Eastern Europe. Credit packages of the leading industrialized nations to the amount of more than \$12 billion over the next few years were announced in July 1990. The Soviet Union received major credits from West Germany. Senior politicians of NATO and the European Community visited Moscow. The conservative British prime minister M. Thatcher stated that the Soviet Union should be brought into closer cooperation with the Group of the Seven industrialized countries and that the European Community should offer membership to the emerging democracies of Eastern Europe 'clearly, openly and generously' (*The Financial Times*, 6 August 1990, p. 1). The European Economic Area (Europäischer Wirtschaftsraum) could provide the grounds for the gradual association of these countries with Western Europe (EC and EFTA). However, the differences among the Western countries as regards the aid packages and a new 'Marshall Plan' for Eastern Europe remain. At the Texas meeting of the Group of Seven in July 1990 a compromise decision was made that the individual countries of the European Community (and particularly Germany and France) could provide larger aid packages, if they wish, to Eastern Europe

The external imbalances of Eastern Europe and particularly of the smaller countries will probably increase in the short term given the new external shocks to their economies: the war in the Gulf associated with rapid rise of oil prices on the world markets, the danger of recession in the West and changes in intra-CMEA payments towards settlements in convertible currencies from 1 January 1991. These factors will put enormous strains on the adjustment policies of Eastern Europe to the new political and economic realities. The Soviet Union will have obviously certain gains from the rise of world oil prices and will further increase its borrowing in the West. All that indicates that clearly defined strategies on how to deal with the debt burden in the Soviet Union and the other Eastern European countries are very important at present. Some Western politicans and economists point to the complexity of the problems involved in this regard for both East and West. The Havard professor J. Sachs (1990, p. 26) stresses that any attempts by the Western countries to collect debts 'would subject Eastern Europe to financial serfdom for the next generation; a plight that would be particularly bitter since the debt is a legacy of communist mismanagement, over which the public had no control'. There is a certain danger that in some of the Eastern European countries the increasing external and internal tensions may result in the fall of the governments implementing the radical economic reforms, and these countries may find themselves under a new form of authoritarian government or with poorly performing (market oriented) economies.

But can one be optimistic that the Eastern European countries will move successfully towards democracy and market economy and will be associated with Europe in the long term? I would suggest an optimistic answer given the potential for economic development in these countries and the favourable climate in East–West relations. As Keynes (1963, p. vii) wrote many years ago: 'if we consistently act on the optimistic hypothesis, this hypothesis will tend to be realized; whilst by acting on the pessimistic hypothesis we can keep ourselves for ever in the pit of want'.

Notes

Introduction

1 The terms 'Eastern Europe', 'CMEA', 'centrally planned economies' are used as synonyms. Eastern Europe refers to the Soviet Union and the six smaller members of the Council for Mutual Economic Assistance (CMEA), also called the Eastern Europe Six, i.e. Bulgaria, Czechoslovakia, the GDR, Hungary, Poland and Romania.

1 Eastern Europe in a time of change

1 It is not my goal to analyse the theoretical attempts of scholars in both the East and West regarding the problems of the present economic reforms. Some interesting publications on this issue are: Jan Adam, *Economic Reforms in the Soviet Union and Eastern Europe since the 1960s*, Macmillan, London, 1989; Abel Aganbegyan, *The Economic Challenge of Perestroika*, Indiana University Press, Indiana, 1988; Abel Aganbegyan, *The Challenge: Economics of Perestroika*, The Second World, London, 1988; Abel Aganbegyan, *Inside Perestroika. The Future of the Soviet Economy*, Harper and Row, New York, 1989; Abel Aganbegyan and Timor Timofeyev, *The New Stage of Perestroika*, Institute for East–West Security Studies, New York, 1988; John Kenneth Galbraith and Stanislaw Menshikov, *Capitalism, Communism and Coexistence*, Hamish Hamilton, London, 1989; Ed A. Hewett, *Reforming the Soviet Economy*, Brookings Institution, Washington, D.C., 1988; Christine Kessides *et al.* (eds.), *Financial Reform in Socialist Economies*, The World Bank, Washington, D.C. 1989.

2 The prominent former Harvard professor, Z. Brzezinski, national security advisor to President Carter, has observed that 'political liberalisation with economic retrogression is a classic formula for revolution' (Z. Brzezinski cited in Sir Geoffrey Howe, 'Soviet foreign policy under Gorbachev', *The World Today*, March 1989, pp. 40–5, p. 44).

3 In the late 1920s the Soviet Union retreated from its so-called 'New Economic Policy' (NEP) which encouraged market relations in the period after 1921. The NEP was replaced by the rigid system of central planning.

4 During 1989 works by the prominent Soviet economist N. Bukharin, who advocated the New Economic Policy in the 1920s and was killed by Stalin,

were published again in the Soviet Union after more than half a century. Bukharin's criticism of Stalinist methods even before they became an orthodoxy has become a source of inspiration and justification for similar critics today. Bukharin wished to maintain a mixed economy for the Soviet Union into the 1930s with a continuing major role for market relations in the allocation of national resources. He took a more tolerant view of the Russian peasantry and the forced collectivisation than Stalin and wanted a more limited role for the state in the transformation of the Soviet Union into a socialist society. In the other Eastern European countries works were also published with provocative ideas on reforming the economy and on 'market socialism'. Among them I want to mention here the works of the Hungarian economist Tibor Liska on 'entrepreneurial socialism'. The Liska model is a competitive market economy, open to international trade and with little state intervention in the economy, where most or even all the means of production are state owned; state enterprises employ wage labour or are leased out to individuals and cooperative firms. All of this indicates that there are signs of radical new ideas in Eastern European economic thought.

5 The 1968 reform envisaged that enterprises would be self-managed and would operate according to supply and demand; they would have various revenues of their own at their disposal. Prices were rationalised in 1967 and it was planned that they would thereafter be market-clearing. The Soviet intervention in Czechoslovakia in August 1968 prevented the real- isation of the liberal goals of the 'Prague Spring'.

6 Franticek Vencovsky, 'Economic prerequisites of freely convertible cur- rency', in *Czechoslovak Economic Digest, Commentaries, Essays*, no. 1, 1989, pp. 57–84, p. 84.

7 It is expected that some 60,000 workers might lose their jobs in 1989–90 because of the restructuring of the economy (*The Financial Times*, 15 October 1988, p. 2). Cuts in the defence industry have also cost many jobs in Hungary (*The Financial Times*, 14 February 1989, p. 2).

8 In the Soviet Union the old system of compulsory deliveries at fixed prices 'does not work' and the losses in agricultural production amount to one- third of total production, according to Soviet Professor Skorov (public lecture, Oxford University, February 1989). More than 20 per cent of Soviet agricultural enterprises failed to fulfil contractual obligations in 1988 and the figures for waste in grain and dairy production were 30 per cent and 45 per cent respectively. More than 200 major Soviet agricultural enterprises, including state farms, collective farms and food processing plants were declared insolvent in 1988 (*The Financial Times*, 1 December 1988, p. 40).

According to the US Department of Agriculture the Soviet grain harvest was much larger than expected and grain imports were reduced by 2 million tonnes to 35 million tonnes in 1989. (*The Financial Times*, 14 October 1989, p. 2). It is not clear, however, if the main force behind this result is the reform in Soviet agriculture. The Soviet prime minister stated in May 1990 that actually the attempts to boost domestic grain production with hard currency payments 'had failed' (*The Financial Times*, 26/7 May 1990, p. 1).

9 Soviet Professor Skorov stated that actually 'we do not know how to change the price system', in a public lecture in Oxford University, February 1989.

10 Josef Zieleniec, 'The current reform process in the Czechoslovak economy and self-management', unpublished manuscript, 1988, p. 5.

11 There is little evidence that these problems have been solved and do not exist at present in Hungary, and the same applies to the other reform-minded Eastern European countries: the Soviet Union, Poland, Bulgaria and Czechoslovakia.

12 Agnes Matits, 'The distribution of profits in Hungarian enterprises', unpublished manuscript, January 1989.

13 It is interesting to mention here de Tocqueville's dictum that the most dangerous time for an authoritarian regime is when it begins to reform itself.

14 Sir Geoffrey Howe, 'Soviet foreign policy under Gorbachev', *The World Today*, March 1989, pp. 40–5.

15 It is not my goal to analyse in detail the foreign trade reforms in Eastern Europe. Some of the interesting publications on this issue are: Aganbegyan and Timofeyev *New Stage of Perestroika* (1988); Yuri Shirjaev, 'Problemi gosudarstvenovo regulirovania vneshneekonomiceskih svjazei' (Problems of the state regulation of the foreign economic relations), in *Planovoe hozajistvo* (Moscow), 2(1989), pp. 114–19; Documents on the reorganization of the USSR foreign economic ties, *Foreign Trade* (Moscow), 5(1987); 'Banks in the socialist countries' foreign economic ties', *Foreign Trade*, 5(1988); 'Domestic and foreign trade prices: their interconnection in the new economic management conditions', *Foreign Trade*, 7(1988); 'Monetary instruments: problems of their improvement', *Foreign Trade*, 4(1988); 'Organization of the USSR's international payments', *Foreign Trade*, 4(1988); 'The USSR banking reform', *Foreign Trade*, 3(1988); 'Foreign economic relations: Currency Aspects', *Foreign Trade*, 1(1989); Martin Koehler, 'Die Geschaeftsbanken im reformierten ungarischen Bankensystem', *Osteuropa-Wirtschaft*, 4(1988), pp. 306–18; Wolf (1988) and many others.

16 *Foreign Trade* (Moscow), 4(1988), p. 5.

17 Vladislav Malkevich, 'East–West economic relations and their prospects', *Foreign Trade* (Moscow), 1(1989), pp. 25–8.

18 See for more details, *Foreign Trade* (Moscow), 3(1988), pp. 40–2.

19 J. Berliner describes the centrally planned economies in the Soviet Union and Eastern Europe as 'documonetary': domestic firms can only use finance for purposes specified in plan documents (Joseph S. Berliner, *The Innovation Decision in Soviet Industry*, MIT Press, Cambridge, Mass., 1976).

20 The total of issued shares should not exceed 50 per cent of the firm's assets. The shares bought by workers should be limited to a maximum of roubles 10,000 per person and would not carry any special voting rights; the total of

such shares should not exceed 30 per cent of the firm's assets (*The Financial Times*, 2 November 1988, p. 2).

2 The Eastern European external debt situation

1 Eastern Europe like many other developing countries experienced balance of payments problems in the 1930s (the Soviet Union, Poland, Hungary, Romania) as well as in the postwar period. The Soviet Union's balance of payments problems in 1929–32 were caused by very heavy machinery imports, deteriorated terms of trade and a drop in agricultural production due to collectivization; a bad harvest was the main reason for problems in 1946 and 1963. The convertible-currency balance of payments difficulties in Hungary (1954–5, 1957) and Czechoslovakia (1962–3) were a result of over-investment in unproductive factories, inefficient allocation of investment funds, collectivization and excessive foreign aid (from Czechoslovakia) (Wiles, *Communist International Economics*, p. 86).

2 The analysis of debt developments in CMEA countries in the present study is based on Western estimates because the official statistics available on Poland, Romania and Hungary are often inadequate. There are some differences in the Western estimates on Eastern European debt (e.g. OECD Secretariat, PlanEcon, CIA, Morgan Guaranty Trust); these differences are not discussed here because they do not materially affect the analysis of debt developments.

3 For a detailed analysis of Eastern Europe's debt in the 1970s and early 1980s see Iliana Zloch-Christy, *Debt Problems of Eastern Europe*, Cambridge University Press, 1988, chapter 2.

4 For an analysis of the macroeconomic adjustment see Zloch-Christy, *Debt Problems*, pp. 90–8.

5 The Romanian authorities published in November 1988 a decree indicating further reducing and rationing the supply of food and energy to households during the winter of 1988/9 (*The Financial Times*, 8 November 1988, p. 2).

6 See United Nations Economic Commission for Europe, *Economic Bulletin for Europe*, 1988, p. 741.

7 For the terms of the rescheduling agreements 1982–6, see Zloch-Christy, *Debt Problems*, pp. 107–8.

8 See *Deficits and Detente*, The Twentieth Century Fund, New York, 1983, p. 7.

9 One may speculate that after almost eight years of austerity policy and restricted borrowing in the West, Romania considered certain changes in its borrowing policy in the late 1980s. One indication was the official visit of Ceausescu in Australia (*The Financial Times*, 12 April 1988, p. 9).

10 The Soviet economist Shmelev stressed in an article some years ago that technico-economic independence is a main factor determining the international economic relations of the Soviet Union (N. Shmelev, 'Krediti i politika', *Mezdunarodnaja Zhizn*, no. 3 (1984), pp. 82–91, p. 91).

11 Economic Commission for Europe, *Economic Bulletin for Europe*, 1988, p. 758.

12 OECD, *Financial Market Trends*, no. 39, February 1988, p. 32.
13 J. Fekete, 'Financing of East–West trade and cooperation 1986–1990', paper presented at conference 'New Horizons in East–West trade and cooperation', Vienna, June 16–19, 1986, p. 9.
14 K. Schroeder, 'Die Ost–West Finanzbeziehungen vor neuen Herausforderungen. Kreditwuerdigkeit, Kapitalverwendung, Exportfaehigkeit', *Osteuropa*, no. 3 (1988), pp. 189–204, p. 198.

3 The financing of East–West trade

1 For a discussion on financing of East–West trade in the 1970s and in the first half of the 1980s, see e.g., Iliana Zloch, *Kredit- und Finanzierungsfragen im Ost–West Handel*, Bundesministerium fur Wissenschaft und Forschung (Vienna), 1985, chapter 4.
2 Some of the recently published books on countertrade are: Berndt R. Samsinger, *Countertrade – Eine alternative Marketing-Strategie*, Paul Haupt Verlag, Bern, 1986; R. Buergin, *Countertrade, eine theoretische und empirische Analyse aus der Sicht einer kleinen offenen Volkswirtschaft*, Peter Lang Verlag, Bern, 1986.
3 United Nations, 'Countertrade in developing countries', in *Supplement to World Economic Survey 1985–1986*, New York, 1986, pp. 52–87, p. 55.
4 *Countertrade. Developing Country Practices*, OECD, Paris, 1985, p. 11.
5 GATT and the International Monetary Fund does not favour countertrade arrangements which they regard as a breach of the multilateral trading system. In a 1983 IMF report it was stated that 'some of the more common and serious disadvantages generally encountered in countertrade arrangements are: (1) a limited choice of products or services that are available for trading at internationally competitive prices; (2) poor quality of goods; (3) the difficulty of marketing products that are not directly consumed by the buyer, especially when the seller places geographical or commercial restrictions on the marketing products; (4) a higher product cost resulting from payments of commissions or fees to the middleman handling sales of products and from bridge financing that may be required owing to long delivery dates'. International Monetary Fund, *Annual Report on Exchange Arrangements and Exchange Restrictions*, Washington, D.C., 1983, p. 46.
6 For example, in the OECD classification, buy-backs are regarded as a form of production compensation (*Countertrade*, OECD, 1985, p. 30).
7 There are many publications on East–West joint ventures. See among others United Nations, Economic Commission for Europe, *East–West Joint Ventures: Economic, Business, Financial and Legal Aspects*, Geneva, 1988; The USSR Chamber of Commerce and Industry and the International Chamber of Commerce (eds.), *Guide to Joint Ventures in the USSR*, 1988; Ernst and Whinney, *Doing Business in the USSR*, London, 1988; Aganbegyan *Inside Perestroika*, (pp. 197–209); and others.
8 According to a Soviet analysis the volume of foreign investment attracted to Eastern Europe by mid-1988 did not exceed $400–500 million, which represents only 0.1–0.2 per cent of their basic productive assets (L. Rodina,

'Socialist-capitalist joint ventures', *Foreign Trade* (Moscow), no. 10 (1988), pp. 12–17, p. 15).

9 Andrew Seton, 'Joint ventures: a new opportunity', in materials of the international conference on *Securing Business with the U.S.S.R.*, held in London, 29–30 September 1988, Institute for International Research.

10 It is not a goal of my analysis to discuss major legal issues in joint venture contracts and the feasibility studies required by the Soviet Union and the other Eastern European countries. For more details see the individual CMEA countries' laws for foreign investments and, for example, materials of the international conference in London, cited in note 9.

11 Joint Economic Committee, US Congress, *Allocation of Resources in the Soviet Union and China – 1987*, USGPO, Washington, D.C. 1989, p. 95.

12 Some of the signed contracts in 1988–9 are: five giant joint ventures in the petrochemical industry (that could double Soviet petrochemical exports by mid-1990s) with a group of Western firms led by Combustion Engineering Inc. (*International Business Week*, 27 March 1989, p. 18); joint venture agreement for petroleum products, food processing plants, magnetic discs by Kodak and others, between the Soviet Union and international consortium of firms (USA and Japan) (*The Financial Times*, 10 November 1988, p. 7); joint venture for chemical equipment production between the Soviet Union and the American firm Occidental Petroleum and the Italian firm Montedison (*Der Spiegel*, 17 October 1988, p. 136); British–Soviet trade centre joint venture in Moscow (*The Financial Times*, 6 April 1989, p. 6); a joint venture between 'Pigment', a Soviet paint manufacturer and the American ICI, the world's largest paint manufacturer (*The Financial Times*, 20 October 1989, p. 3); and many others.

13 See for a discussion of cooperation agreements in the 1970s and the first half of the 1980s, Zloch, *Kredit-*, pp. 101–3.

14 See *ibid.*, p. 103.

15 For the role of licensing see Ryszard Rapacki, 'The role of licensing in the strategy of Western firms in centrally planned economies, *Osteuropa Wirtschaft*, 1(1989), pp. 49–61.

16 *The Journal of the British–Soviet Chamber of Commerce*, no. 8 (1988), p. 6.

17 For a discussion on clearing/switch and 'transit' deals in the 1970s and early 1980s, see I. Zloch, 'Finanzierungsformen im Ost–West Handel,' in *Osteuropa Wirtschaft*, no. 2 (1986), Munich.

18 Economic Commission for Europe, *Economic Survey of Europe in 1986–87*, New York, 1987, p. 258.

19 Forfeited claims are traded on a discount basis at fixed rates and the latter are based upon the cost of borrowing in the interbank Euromarkets.

20 OECD, *Financial Market Trends*, 'East–West financial relations: recent developments and medium-term prospects', no. 39 (1988), p. 32.

21 See Zloch *Kredit-*, chapters 4 and 6 (for Austria); Zloch (1986) 'Finanzierungsformen im Ost–West Handel',); I. Zloch, 'Die Verschuldung der Oststaaten in Osterreich', *Wirtschaft und Gesellschaft*, no. 4 (1985), Vienna; Zloch-Christy, *Debt Problems*.

22 Zloch, 'Die Verschuldung der Oststaaten in Osterreich'.

23 For an analysis of IMF and World Bank lending to Eastern Europe in 1982–6, see Zloch-Christy, *Debt Problems*, pp. 118–27, 129–32.

24 Ceausescu, the Romanian leader, announced in a speech in April 1989 that his country had 'completely repaid' the foreign debts (*The Financial Times*, 17 April 1989, p. 2). It is not clear, however, if this statement referred to commercial banks' debt only or to government and financial institutions' debt obligations as well.

25 See I. Zloch, 'Developing countries' access to the international securities markets', World Bank ED Staff Working Papers, no. 2 (1987), Washington, D.C.

4 Medium- and long-term debt prospects in Eastern Europe

1 Cited in Holzman 'CMEA hard-currency deficits', p. 144.

2 The prospective ability of a nation to transform its economy in such a way as to improve the balance of payments situation and/or repay its debts.

3 Aganbegyan and Timofeyev, *New Stage of Perestroika*, p. 43.

4 A 1 per cent rise in interest rates would result in an approximately $500 million increase in external payments for Poland (if agreement on debt reduction were not achieved with the Western commercial bank and Paris Club creditors in the early 1990s).

5 For further discussion see Zloch-Christy, *Debt Problems*, pp. 15–26; Jozef M. van Brabant, *Adjustment, Structural Change and Economic Efficiency. Aspects of Monetary Cooperation in Eastern Europe*, Cambridge University Press, New York and Cambridge, 1987, pp. 123–6, 399–403.

6 Fekete cited in Holzman 'CMEA hard-currency deficits', p. 160.

7 See Gomulka and Nove, *East–West Technology Transfer*, pp. 35–7.

8 The Soviet newspaper *Izvestia* published in October 1988 a report of Goskomstat, the Central Statistical Committee, on loss-making enterprises in the Soviet economy in 1987. According to this report 3,960 industrial enterprises, or 13 per cent of the total, were loss-making. Some of the reasons cited by *Izvestia* for the losses are 'elementary and bad management'; failure of the central planning authorities to balance supply and demand both for raw materials and finished products; poor technology of production; and lack of coordination (*The Financial Times*, 4 October 1988, p. 2).

9 The Soviet economic journal *EKO* published an analysis in early 1989 showing that among 216 major export items, including machine tools, cars and diesel engines, only 20 met the demands of the world market; only 29 per cent of engineering products and 14 per cent of machine tools respectively, match international standards. Machinery and equipment represent only 13 per cent of total Soviet exports at present, from a level above 20 per cent in the early 1980s. The Soviet engineering exports are failing to compete on world markets according to *EKO*, because of poor quality, shoddy finishing, and a failure to observe international technical standards (*The Financial Times*, 6 January 1989, p. 4).

10 For a discussion, see Zloch-Christy, *Debt Problems*, pp. 19–21.

11 For a discussion, see, Holzman, *Foreign Trade*, Zloch-Christy, *Debt problems*, pp. 22–6.

12 Market-oriented reforms fail to achieve more effectiveness when party and state bureaucracy play a dominant role in the economic behaviour patterns and profit distribution.

13 Kornai, 'The Hungarian reform process', *Journal of Economic Literature*, December 1986, p. 1687.

14 For a discussion, see J. Kornai, *Economics of Shortage*, Amsterdam, North-Holland, 1980.

15 The more profit depends on bureaucratic intervention the less is the role of the market.

16 General problems of country risk analysis in lending to Western Europe are discussed in some of the previous publications by the author: Zloch-Christy, *Debt Problems*, ch. 6.

17 In intra-CMEA trade, so-called contract prices, expressed in transferable roubles, are applied; the contract prices are not based on domestic prices in the CMEA countries, but are 'adjusted' world market prices using a moving five-year price formula.

18 Barry Eichengreen and Richard Portes, 'Dealing with debts: the 1930s and the 1980s', Discussion Paper no. 300, Centre for Economic Policy Research, February 1989, pp. 35–6.

19 'Buying our Debts Back', in *Prawo i Zycie*, no. 46, 12 November 1988, cited in *Economic Review* of British and American Embassies in Warsaw, 18 November 1988, pp. 10–14; *The Financial Times*, 5 October 1989, p. 3.

20 R. Portes 'Economic reforms, international capital flows and the development of the domestic capital markets in CPEs', *European Economic Review*, vol. 33, no. 2/3, p. 469.

21 As regards the progress of the Hungarian political and economic reform in the late 1980s it is worth noting the statement made by the well-known Hungarian economist Martin Tardos that 'Western bankers like to hear rhetoric about radical economic denationalization and market economy, because of our debt but the communist party knows that if it does what it says it will lose power' (*The Financial Times*, 14 April 1989, p. 3).

22 A team from the International Monetary Fund held negotiations in Warsaw on terms of credit to Poland during 1989 and 1990. Poland received the first IMF and World Bank funds in early 1990. In West Germany, Poland's major creditor, there were proposals for debt relief and rescheduling of the Polish debt in the late 1980s. The former West German Federal Chancellor in the 1970s, Helmut Schmidt, stated in early 1989 that: 'I am in favour of rescheduling the Polish debt and of offering Poland terms of repayment that its economy will be able to bear; I am speaking of payment of credits granted to Poland by Western governments and by private banks, other financial institutions, consortia and firms' (*Trybuna Ludu*, no. 65, March 17, 1989, p. 5, cited in *Polish News Bulletin of the British and American Embassies* in Warsaw, March 17, 1989, p. 16). The American President, George Bush, stated in April 1989 that his administration was ready to provide trade credits to Poland and that there was a discussion on

a more sympathetic attitude to Polish debt rescheduling and American support for limited involvement by the IMF in Eastern Europe, including Poland (*The Financial Times*, 13 April 1989, p. 8). He also suggested provision of loans by the International Finance Corporation to Poland, US selective tariff relief for Polish exports, Paris Club rescheduling of Polish debt and other debt relief measures (*The Financial Times*, 18 April 1989, p. 28). The United Kingdom announced in April 1989 that it would provide new credits to Poland in the future. As discussed in chapter 1 and chapter 2, several Western countries announced aid packages for Poland and Hungary in late 1989 in support of their programmes for political and economic liberalization.

Conclusion

1 Janos Kornai, 'Comments on the papers prepared in the World Bank about socialist countries', unpublished manuscript 1984, p. 3.
2 J. M. Keynes, *The Economic Consequences of the Peace*, Macmillan, London, 1919, vol. 2 of *The Collected Writing of John Maynard Keynes*, Macmillan and Cambridge, Cambridge University Press, Cambridge, 1982, p. 178.

References

Adam, Jan (1989) *Economic Reforms in the Soviet Union and Eastern Europe, since the 1960s*, London, Macmillan.

Aganbegyan, Abel (1988) *The Economic Challenge of Perestroika*, Indiana, Indiana University Press.

(1988a) *The Challenge: Economics of Perestroika*, London, The Second World.

(1989) *Inside Perestroika. The Future of the Soviet Economy*, Harper and Row, New York, 1989.

Aganbegyan, Abel, and Timofeyev, Timor (1988b) *The New Stage of Perestroika*, New York, Institute for East–West Security Studies.

Anikin, A. (1989) USSR: Financial crisis and international monetary policy, unpublished manuscript.

Business International SA, (June 1985) *IOI Checklists for Coping with Worldwide Countertrade Problems*, Geneva.

BIS, *International Banking and Financial Market Developments*, Basle, various years.

Deutsches Institut für Wirtschaftsforschung, *Wochenbericht*, Berlin (West), various issues.

Doronin, I. (1988) 'Problemy sovershenstrovanija valjutno-finansovich instrumentov, *Vneshnaja Torgovlja SSSR* (Moscow), 4: 42–5; 6: 35–9.

Duwendag, Dieter (1987) *Capital Flight from Developing Countries: Estimates and Determinants for 25 Major Borrowers*, SUERF, Tilburg, Netherlands.

Ekonomiceskaja gazeta, Moscow, various issues.

The Economist, London, various issues.,

Fekete, Janos (1982) *Back to the Realities: Reflections of Hungarian Banker*, Budapest, Akademiai Kiado.

(1986) 'Financing of East–West trade and cooperation 1986–1990', paper presented at the conference 'New Horizons in East–West Trade and Cooperation', Vienna, June 16–19.

The Financial Times, London, various issues.

Fisher, Bart S., and Harte, Kathleen M. (eds.) (1985) *Barter in the World Economy*, New York, Praeger.

Foreign Trade, Moscow, various issues.

Galbraith, John Kenneth, and Stanislaw Menshikov (1989) *Capitalism, Communism and Coexistence*, London, Hamish Hamilton.

GATT (1984) 'Countertrade' (CG.18/W/80), Geneva.

Generale Bank (1985) 'De compensatie – Een praktiik die aanslaat', *Rechtstreeks vanuit de Wereldmarkt*, September 1985, pp. 4–7.

Geron, Leonard (1989) *Joint Ventures in the USSR Data Base*, London, Royal Institute of International Affairs.

Gomulka, Stanislaw, and Alex Nove (1984) *East–West Technology Transfer*, Paris, OECD.

Hewett, Ed A. (1988) *Reforming the Soviet Economy*, Washington, D.C., Brookings Institution.

Holzman, Franklyn D. (1974) *Foreign Trade under Central Planning*, Cambridge Mass., Harvard University Press.

(1978) 'CMEA hard currency deficits and rouble convertibility,' in Nita G. Watts (1978), *Economic Relations between East and West*, London, Macmillan.

International Monetary Fund Survey, Washington, D.C., various issues.

World Economic Outlook, various issues.

Janiszewski, H. A. (1983) 'Restrictive provisions in licensing agreements in Poland', *Journal of World Trade Law*, 17 (2): 154–8.

Jones, Stephen F. (1984) *North–South Countertrade*, Special Report no. 174, London, The Economist Intelligence Unit.

Kalecki, Michal (1972) *Selected Essays on the Economic Growth of the Socialist and the Mixed Economy*, Cambridge, Cambridge University Press.

Kaser, Michael C. (1988) 'The reform of foreign economic relations', unpublished manuscript.

(1988a) 'The Sino-Soviet model in the context of socialist system reform', paper presented at the conference on 'Alternative Models of Socialist Economic Systems', Gyor, 18–22 March.

Keynes, J. M. (1963) *Essays in Persuasion*, New York, The Norton Library.

Kindleberger, Charles P. (1968) *International Economics* (4th edn), Homewood, Ill., Richard D. Irwin.

Konstantinov, Juri (1989) 'Konvertiruemost rublja: konzeptualnii podhod', *Voprosi Ekonomiki* (Moscow), 9: 33–40.

Kornai, Janos (1980) *Economics of Shortage*, Amsterdam, North-Holland.

(1984) 'Comments on the papers prepared in the World Bank about socialist countries', unpublished manuscript, 1984.

(1989) 'The affinity between ownership and coordination mechanisms. The common experiences of reform in socialist countries', paper presented at the conference on 'Market Forces in Planned Economies', Moscow, 28–30 March.

(1986) 'The Hungarian reform process: visions, hopes and reality', *Journal of Economic Literature*, December, pp. 1687–737.

(1990) 'The Road to a Free Economy. Shifting from a Socialist System: The Case of Hungary', Cambridge M.A.

Kuznetsov, I. (1988) 'Byt' li u nas valutnomu rinku', *Ekonomicheskaja Gazeta* (Moscow), 26: 21.

de Lombaerde, P. (1988) 'Kompensatietechnieken in de Oost–Westhandel', *The South African Journal of Economics*, 56 (4), December.

McVey, Thomas B. (1988) 'Countertrade: commercial practices, legal issues and policy dilemmas', *Law and Policy in International Business*, 16 (1), Washington, D.C., Georgetown University.

Matits, Agnes (1989) *The Socialist Reform Process and Measuring its Success with Illustrations from Hungarian Experience*, Budapest, Karl Marx University of Economics.

Nuti, Domenico Mario (1989) 'Remonetisation and capital markets in the reform of centrally planned economies', *European Economic Review*, 33: 427–38.

OECD (1985) *Countertrade: Developing Country Practices*, Paris.

OECD, *Financial Market Trends*, various issues, Paris.

OECD/BIS, *Statistics on External Indebtedness: Bank and Trade Related Non-Bank External Claims on Individual Borrowing Countries and Territories*, Paris and Basle, various issues.

Osteuropa Wirtschaft, Munich, various issues.

Parsons, John E. (1985) *A theory of Countertrade Financing of International Business*, Working Paper 1632–85, Cambridge, Mass., MIT.

Pissula, Petra (1988) 'Das Verhältnis der Sowjetunion zum GATT und zum Internationalen Währungsfonds', *Osteuropa-Wirtschaft*, 33 (4): 319–26.

Portes, Richard (1983) 'The Soviet balance of payments constraint', in Twentieth Century Fund, pp. 13–92.

(1989) 'Economic reforms, international capital flows and the development of the domestic capital markets in CPEs', *European Economic Review*, 33, (2/3): 466–71.

Pravda, Moscow, various issues.

Sachs, Jeffrey (1990) 'What is to be done?', *The Economist*, 13 January, 21–6.

Tardos, Martin (1989) 'Reforms or transforming the system', unpublished manuscript.

(1989a) 'The Hungarian banking reform', unpublished manuscript.

Twentieth Century Fund (1983) *Deficits and Détente: Report of an International Conference on the Balance of Trade in the Comecon Countries*, New York.

United Nations (1986) 'Countertrade in developing countries', in *Supplement to World Economic Survey 1985–1986*, New York.

United Nations, ECE, *Economic Bulletin for Europe*, Geneva, various issues.

(1988) *East–West Joint Ventures: Economic, Business, Financial and Legal Aspects*, Geneva.

US Congress, Joint Economic Committee (1988) *Allocation of Resources in the Soviet Union and China – 1987*, Washington, D.C., USGPO.

van Brabant, Jozef M. (1987) *Adjustment, Structural Change and Economic Efficiency. Aspects of Monetary Cooperation in Eastern Europe*, Cambridge University Press, New York and Cambridge.

Verzariu, Pompiliu (1985) *Countertrade, Barter, Offsets: New Strategies for Profit in International Trade*, New York, McGraw-Hill Book Co.

Wall Street Journal, various issues.

Wiles, Peter (1968) *Communist International Economics*, Oxford, Basil Blackwell.

Wolf, Thomas (1988) *Foreign Trade in the Centrally Planned Economy*, Harwood Academic Publishers, New York.

World Bank, *World Bank Annual Report*, Washington, D.C., various issues.

World Financial Markets, New York, Morgan Guaranty Trust Company, various issues.

Zloch, Iliana (1985) *Kredit- und Finanzierungsfragen im Ost–West Handel*, Bundesministerium fur Wissenschaft und Forschung, Vienna.

Zloch-Christy, Iliana (1986) *Hard Currency Debt and the Growth of the Eastern European Economies*, World Bank Staff Working Paper no. 12, December, Washington, D.C.

(1988) *Debt Problems of Eastern Europe*, Cambridge and New York, Cambridge University Press.

(1989) *East European Creditworthiness – 1980–87 and Prospects*, Papers in East European Economics no. 77, University of Oxford.

(1989a) *Programmes for Economic Liberalization and the External Balance in Eastern Europe*, mimeo, International Monetary Fund, Washington, D.C., September.

(1989b) *Capital Flight from Developing Countries: Current Problems and Prospects*, mimeo, International Monetary Fund, Washington, D.C., September.

(1990) '*Some issues on the convertibility of the Eastern European currencies*', Research Study prepared for the United Nations Economic Commission for Europe, Geneva.

Index

adjustment, 41, 46, 102
Aganbegyan, A., 4, 5, 16, 24, 73, 78
agriculture: 16; Hungary, 12; Poland,
10; Soviet Union, 8
Austria, 44, 55, 66

balance of payments, 1, 42, 43;
Hungary, 99
Bank for International Settlements
(BIS), 34
bilateralism, 81
Bogomolov, O., 8
borrowing, 30, 34, 41, 42, 48, 77, 91;
Bulgaria, 33, 41; Czechoslovakia,
33, 98; GDR, 98; Hungary, 36, 41;
Soviet Union, 35, 41, 92, 100; policy
(Eastern European), 48–9; terms,
36; see also debt
Brazil, 79
Bretton Woods institutions, 15, 43, 44,
73, 98; see also International
Monetary Fund, World Bank
Bulgaria, 3, 16, 20, 27; debt, 41, 92, 98;
current accounts, 31, 32; gross
debt, 34; net debt, 34, 35; reform,
14–15, 17, 18; trade balance, 30
bureaucracy, 18, 83, 84, 87
buy-backs (deals), 2, 52,, 56–7, 101; see
also countertrade

capital account, see balance of
payments
capital flight, 40, 99
capital markets; Eastern Europe, 27–9;
Western, 45, 85, 98
Ceausescu, 99
centrally planned controls, 79
centrally planned economy, 82
clearing switch deals, 64–6; see also
'transit' deals
CMEA, see Council for Mutual
Economic Assistance

commercial compensation, 52–7; see
also countertrade, multilateral trade
accords
Commodity convertibility, 24, 62;
non-convertibility, 81
common market, 50
competition, 79
convertibility, see commodity
convertibility; currency
convertibility
cooperation agreements, 63–4, 108
Council for Mutual Economic
Assistance (CMEA), 1, 3, 34, 35,
37, 78, 85, 88–9, 110
counterpurchase, 52, 52–6, 55, 101
countertrade, 2, 52–7, 101
country risk analysis, 85, 110
credit risk, see country risk analysis
creditor–debtor policy strategies,
47–50
credits: bank-to-bank, 49; debt trends,
34–6, 49; export, 36; government,
43; guaranteed, 49; IMF, 35, 44;
World Bank, 73; see also names of
specific countries; loans
creditworthiness, 41, 80, 99; Hungary,
42–7; Poland, 42–7
Cuba, 100
currency; convertibility, 10, 11, 15,
24–5, 62, 83; non-convertibility, 81
current account, 1, 31, 32, 42
Czechoslovakia: debt, 41, 92, 98;
current accounts, 31, 32; gross
debt, 34; net debt, 35; reform, 9–10,
17; securities markets, 75, 98; trade
balance, 30

debt, 30, 34, 35, 40, 77, 98, 110;
crisis, 30, 51, 98, 102; indicators, 36,
99; relief measures, 47, 97, 102;
reschedulings, 45; rouble, 92, 95;
problem, 1, 41, 30–42; prospects,

77–100; situation, 1, 41, 30–50; *see also* borrowing, credits, loans
deflationary policy, 41
detente, 22, 77
devaluation, 12, 25, 81
development, 1, 30; strategy, 78, 82, 101
direct controls, 41, 80
disequilibrium, 30, 102

East Germany, *see* German Democratic Republic (GDR)
economic integration *see* integration
equipment (imported), 96
European Community (EC), 20, 21, 43, 96
European Free Trade area (EFTA), 20, 81
excess demand, 102
exchange rates, 25, 80, 83
export factoring, 2, 68
export leasing, 2, 66–7, 101
exports, 39; net debt ratios, 39
external balance, 47, 91, 102; *see also* balance of payments, current account

Federal Republic of Germany (FRG), 21, *see also* West Germany
Fekete, J., 49
financial compensation, 2, 64–70
foreign borrowing, 40, 77; *see also* borrowing, debt
foreign exchange, 23; auctions, 9, 11, 26
foreign trade mechanism, reforming, 22–7
forfeiting, 2, 52, 68–70, 101
France, 20, 35
free financing, 72–3

GATT, *see* General Agreement on Tariffs and Trade
GDR, *see* German Democratic Republic
General Agreement on Tariffs and Trade, 23, 52, 73, 74, 107
German Democratic Republic (GDR), 1, 21, 50, 59; debt, 41, 92, 98; current accounts, 31, 32; gross debt, 34; net debt, 35; reform, 17; trade balance, 30
Germany, 3; *see also* Federal Republic of Germany; German Democratic Republic
Gorbachev, M., 5
growth, 102; -cum-debt economic policy, 49

Hungary: debt, 41, 92, 99; creditworthiness, 43, 99; current accounts, 31; gross debt, 34; net debt, 35t; reform, 12–4, 17; securities markets, 75; Soviet trade, 96; trade balance, 30

imports, 79; liquidity ratios, 40; restrictions on Western, 48, 49; Soviet, 47
inconvertibility, *see* commodity non-convertibility; currency non-convertibility
India, 94
inflation, 16
innovation, 81
insolvency, 41, 46
integration, 89
interest rates, 11, 79, 83, 109
international organizations, *see also* Bretton Woods institutions, IMF, World Bank
investment, 17, 84; foreign, 8
Iran, 94
Italy, 21, 35, 48

Japan, 44, 48
joint ventures, 2, 57–63, 101

Keynes, J. M., 5, 102
Konstantinov, 25
Kornai, J., 7, 83, 101

labour, 7
Latin America, 94; debtor countries, 41
leadership, 86
lending, 47, 48; political risk assessment, 84–91
licence contracts, 63
lines of credit, 70, 72
liquidity: difficulties, 41, 47, 49, 100; problems, 46; squeezes, 98
loans, 43, 44, 48, 86; *see also* credits

market, 8
Marshall Plans, 21
most favoured nation status, 93
multilateral trade accords, 57
multilateralism, 26

oil: exports (Soviet Union), 94; prices, 79, 92, 93, 94; production (Soviet Union), 94

Paris Club, 43, 45
perestroika policy, 85

Poland: debt, 41, 92, 99;
  creditworthiness, 42, 99; current
  accounts, 31; gross debt, 34; net
  debt, 35; reform, 10–2, 17; trade
  balance, 30
policy: creditor–debtor (East–West),
  47, 50; *see also* creditor–debtor
  policy strategies
political risk assessment, 84–91
production compensation, 2, 52, 57–64
project financing, 70, 71–2

ratios: debt service, 39; liquidity, 40;
  net debt exports, 39
recession, 79
refinancing (Hungary), 41, 44
reform, 17; dilemmas, 6–7; pillars,
  4–5; *see also* names of specific
  countries
Romania, 3; debt, 42, 92, 99–100;
  current accounts, 32; gross debt, 34;
  net debt, 35; reform, 17; trade
  balance, 30

Sachs, Jeffrey, 45
savings-investment gap, 77
scenarios: alternative, 91–100
securities: markets, 2, 52, 74–6;
  offerings, 75; *see also* names of
  specific countries
social conditions, 89–90
Soviet allies
Soviet Union: debt, 41, 92, 100; current
  accounts, 32; gross debt 34; IMF

and World Bank, 23, 73–4, 102; net
  debt, 35; reform, 7–9, 17; foreign
  trade, 22–7; securities markets, 75,
  100; trade balance, 30
structural changes: Hungary, 46;
  Poland, 11
supplier's credits, 70–1
switch, *see* clearing switch deals

tariffs, 23, 93
tax policy, 84; reforms, 11
technology: CMEA, 96; Western, 81,
  96
terms of trade, 79; in East–West trade,
  33
transfer problem, 78
transferable rouble (TR), 27, 78, 81,
  110; *see also* currency
transit deals, 64–6; *see also* clearing
  switch deals
triangular compensation, 65, 66

United Kingdom, 12, 20, 21, 36, 43, 48
United States (USA), 19, 21, 43, 44, 48,
  74
unemployment, 79

wages, 84
West Germany, 20, 21, 35, 48, 55, 58;
  see also Federal Republic of
  Germany
World Bank, 23, 73, 74; *see also* Bretton
  Woods institutions, international
  organizations

Soviet and East European Studies

62 BENJAMIN PINKUS
The Jews of the Soviet Union
The history of a national minority

61 FRANCESCO BENVENUTI
The Bolsheviks and the Red Army, 1918–1922

60 HIROAKI KUROMIYA
Stalin's industrial revolution
Politics and workers, 1928–1932

59 LEWIS SIEGELBAUM
Stakhanovism and the politics of productivity in the USSR, 1935–1941

58 JOZEF M. VAN BRABANT
Adjustment, structural change and economic efficiency
Aspects of monetary cooperation in Eastern Europe

57 ILIANA ZLOCH-CHRISTY
Debt problems of Eastern Europe

56 SUSAN BRIDGER
Women in the Soviet countryside
Women's roles in rural development in the Soviet Union

55 ALLEN LYNCH
The Soviet study of international relations

54 DAVID GRANICK
Job rights in the Soviet Union: their consequences

53 ANITA PRAŻMOWSKA
Britain, Poland and the Eastern Front, 1939

52 ELLEN JONES AND FRED GRUPP
Modernization, value change and fertility in the Soviet Union

51 CATHERINE ANDREYEV
Vlasov and the Russian liberation movement
Soviet reality and émigré theories

50 STEPHEN WHITE
The origins of détente
The Genoa Conference and Soviet–Western relations 1921–1922

49 JAMES MCADAMS
East Germany and détente
Building authority after the Wall

48 S. G. WHEATCROFT AND R. W. DAVIES (EDS.)
Materials for a balance of the Soviet national economy 1928–1930

47 SYLVANA MALLE
The economic organization of war communism, 1918–1921

46 DAVID S. MASON
Public opinion and political change in Poland, 1980–1982

45 MARK HARRISON
Soviet planning in peace and war 1938–1945

44 NIGEL SWAIN
Collective farms which work?

43 J. ARCH GETTY
Origins of the great purges
The Soviet Communist Party reconsidered, 1933–1938

42 TADEUSZ SWIETOCHOWSKI
Russian Azerbaijan 1905–1920
The shaping of national identity in a muslim community

41 RAY TARAS
Ideology in a socialist state
Poland 1956–1983

50 SAUL ESTRIN
Self-management: economic theory and Yugoslav practice

39 S. A. SMITH
Red Petrograd
Revolution in the factories 1917–1918

38 DAVID A. DYKER
The process of investment in the Soviet Union

36 JEAN WOODALL
The socialist corporation and technocratic power
The Polish United Workers Party, industrial organisation and workforce control 1958–1980

35 WILLIAM J. CONYNGHAM
The modernization of Soviet industrial management

34 ANGELA STENT
From embargo to Ostpolitik
The political economy of West German–Soviet relations 1955–1980

32 BLAIR A. RUBLE
Soviet trade unions
Their development in the 1970s

31 R. F. LESLIE (ED.)
The history of Poland since 1863

30 JOZEF M. VAN BRABANT
Socialist economic integration
Aspects of contemporary economic problems in Eastern Europe

28 STELLA ALEXANDER
Church and state in Yugoslavia since 1945

27 SHEILA FITZPATRICK
Education and social mobility in the Soviet Union 1921–1934

23 PAUL VYSNÝ
Neo-slavism and the Czechs 1898–1914

22 JAMES RIORDAN
Sport in Soviet society
Development of sport and physical education in Russia and the USSR

14 RUDOLF BIĆANIĆ
Economic policy in socialist Yugoslavia

The following series titles are now out of print:

1 ANDREA BOLTHO
Foreign trade criteria in socialist economies

2 SHEILA FITZPATRICK
The commissariat of enlightenment
Soviet organization of education and the arts under Lunacharsky, October 1917–1921

3 DONALD J. MALE
Russian peasant organisation before collectivisation
A study of commune and gathering 1925–1930

4 P. WILES (ED.)
The prediction of communist economic performance

5 VLADIMIR V. KUSIN
The intellectual origins of the Prague Spring
The development of reformist ideas in Czechoslovakia 1956–1967

6 GALIA GOLAN
The Czechoslovak reform movement

7 NAUN JASNY
Soviet economists of the twenties
Names to be remembered

8 ASHA L. DATAR
India's economic relations with the USSR and Eastern Europe, 1953–1969

9 T. M. PODOLSKI
Socialist banking and monetary control
The experience of Poland

10 SHMUEL GALAI
The liberation movement in Russia

11 GALIA GOLAN
Reform rule in Czechoslovakia
The Dubcek era 1968–1969

12 GEOFFREY A. HOSKING
The Russian constitutional experiment
Government and Duma 1907–1914

13 RICHARD B. DAY
Leon Trotsky and the politics of economic isolation
15 JAN M. CIECHANOWSKI
The Warsaw rising of 1944

16 EDWARD A. HEWITT
Foreign trade prices in the Council for Mutual Economic Assistance

17 ALICE TEICHOVA
An economic background to Munich
International business and Czechoslovakia 1918–1938

18 DANIEL F. CALHOUN
The united front: the TUC and the Russians 1923–1928

19 GALIA GOLAN
Yom Kippur and after
The Soviet Union and the Middle East crisis

20 MAUREEN PERRIE
The agrarian policy of the Russian Socialist-Revolutionary Party
From its origins through the revolution of 1905–1907

21 GABRIEL GORODETSKY
The precarious truce: Anglo-Soviet relations 1924–1927

24 GREGORY WALKER
Soviet book publishing policy

25 FELICITY ANN O'DELL
Socialisation through children's literature
The Soviet example

26 T. H. RIGBY
Lenin's government: Sovnarkom 1917–1922

29 MARTIN CAVE
Computers and economic planning
The Soviet experience

33 MARTIN MYANT
Socialism and democracy in Czechoslovakia 1944–1948

37 ISRAEL GETZLER
Kronstadt 1917–1921
The fate of a Soviet democracy